LETTERS
TO MY
MOTHER

LETTERS
TO MY
MOTHER

TRIBUTES TO THE
WOMEN WHO GIVE US
LIFE—AND LOVE

EDITED BY
BARB KARG & RICK SUTHERLAND

ADAMS MEDIA
AVON, MASSACHUSETTS

Published by
Adams Media, an F+W Publications Company
57 Littlefield Street, Avon, MA 02322. U.S.A.
www.adamsmedia.com

ISBN 10: 1-59869-168-6
ISBN 13: 978-1-59869-168-9

Printed in the United States of America.

J I H G F E D C B A

Library of Congress Cataloging-in-Publication Data
is available from the publisher.

This publication is designed to provide accurate and authoritative information
with regard to the subject matter covered. It is sold with the understanding
that the publisher is not engaged in rendering legal, accounting, or other professional advice. If legal advice or other expert assistance is required, the ser-
vices of a competent professional person should be sought.

—From a *Declaration of Principles* jointly adopted by a Committee of the
American Bar Association and a Committee of Publishers and Associations

Many of the designations used by manufacturers and sellers to distinguish their
product are claimed as trademarks. Where those designations appear in this
book and Adams Media was aware of a trademark claim, the designations have
been printed with initial capital letters.

This book is available at quantity discounts for bulk purchases.
For information, please call 1-800-289-0963.

THIS BOOK IS DEDICATED TO our extraordinary family members who continually touch our lives and our hearts: Ma, Pop, Dad, Chris, Glen, Anne, Terry Bob, Kathy, Jeannie and Jim, Jim V., Ellen and Jim, Karla, and the Blonde Bombshell. We love you all.

It is also a tribute to all the mothers of the world who touch our lives on a daily basis. It is because of their love, strength, and courage that we are all better individuals. To all of you, we say thank you.

And to Trudi Karg and Rebecca Sutherland, we love you both more than mere words could even begin to express. We honor you, and thank you for being our mothers.

CONTENTS

3. YOU ARE MY HERO 85

4. YOU ARE ALWAYS IN MY HEART.....................125

ACKNOWLEDGMENTS

Many individuals worked very hard to bring *Letters To My Mother* to fruition. A heartfelt thanks goes out to all our wonderful contributors, who put their heart and soul into writing letters that weren't always easy to write. You did it with grace and aplomb, and we thank you for you willingness to share your mothers with the world.

We'd also like to thank the fine folks at Adams Media for their support and encouragement. Paula Munier is one of the finest individuals we've ever known. As a true friend and a mother, we honor and cherish her for her never-ending wit, intelligence, and ability to love. Thanks go out as well to editor Andrea Norville, an outstanding gal in her own right, for her support, her humor, and her savvy, and to Brendan O'Neill for his dilligent work on the project. We'd also like to give a shout to Laura Daly, Sue Beale, and Brett Palana-Shanahan for their hard work and expertise, and to the designers, Holly Curtis and Colleen Cunningham.

For all her hard work and dedication to *Letters To My Mother*, we offer our unending praise to Jeannie. You're a true star, my dear, and we couldn't have done it without you! And thanks, Ma. As always and forever, you're always here for us.

INTRODUCTION

Mothers are amazing individuals. They are the genesis of our being, the warmth in our soul, and the light that guides us through our lifelong quest to become better people. Mothers are replete with wisdom, practicality, common sense, humor, intelligence, and supreme logic. They take care of us from birth through life. They tend to our every need when we're sick, and they make us smile even during our most trying hours. They stand behind us no matter what we endeavor to accomplish. When we succeed their pride shines as bright as the morning sun, and when we falter they pick us up, enveloping us in love and confidence to try again.

Our race, creed, age, or beliefs have no bearing on our love for our mothers. That love is universal, and it is expressed in our eyes and the eyes of all of our children. The world is a better place because of our mothers. They not only touch our hearts, but the hearts of all those who have the honor of knowing them in their lifetime. It would be unrealistic to say that there aren't turbulent times between mother and child, but in the end that matters little, because no other creature on the planet has the capacity for forgiveness that a mother possesses. Without question and without fail, we are our mothers' children, inexplicably bound together by love, trust, and faith.

This anthology is a testament to all the mothers in our lives who gave us life and love. To the mothers who gave up so much and asked for nothing in return. To all the mothers who love us unconditionally through times of triumph and tribulation. To the mothers who've kept us safe from harm, and guided our way through dark nights and foggy morns. To all of our mothers, we pay homage and can say, unreservedly, "We love you."

Like its predecessor, *Letters To My Teacher*, *Letters To My Mother* is a labor of love. It was always our intent to pay tribute to mothers of the world in the best way we knew how. Mothers are often not given the credit they deserve, and while this book offers but a small measure of praise, it is our fondest hope that mothers everywhere will read these letters and know how much they are loved and cherished.

To all of the outstanding individuals who contributed to this book, and to all those who took the time to send in wonderful letters, we salute you. All of you shared with us the amazing strength, courage, triumph, tragedy, and unconditional love your mothers have shown you, and to put it quite simply, what all of you wrote was nothing short of extraordinary. From the bottom of our hearts, we thank you all. We know your mothers would all be very proud.

In doing this anthology, we pay tribute to our own mothers as well. Trudi Karg and Rebecca Sutherland have played a huge role in our development as human beings. Moms, both of you, through your unending love, encouragement, unconditional support, intelligence, humor, and grace, you have made us proud to be the individuals we've become. Because of you, we live with our hopes and dreams, and the knowledge that whatever we do in this lifetime or the next, you will forever remain by our sides. We love you, we honor you, and we thank you for being our mothers.

Barb Karg and Rick Sutherland

I.

You Are My Inspiration

Throughout history, mothers have proven to be the most inspirational individuals on the planet. They are selfless and caring by their very nature, and encourage us no matter our journey or its outcome. With a mother's unending support, a person can accomplish anything in life and know that there is one person whom they can trust, whom they will never disappoint.

Our mothers serve as the ultimate example of how we live our lives. They work to make our existence better, to show us that with patience and perseverance we can be anyone we want to be and do anything we want to do. In some cases they raise us alone, sacrificing their own wants and desires, showing us the meaning of what it is to be truly unselfish.

Mothers reinvent themselves through their children, perhaps out of necessity, or because when they look into their children's eyes, they see themselves. As women, our mothers work tirelessly to assure that we never lack the essentials of life, and they do it with a smile in their heart and a spirit that overcomes all measure of forgiveness. They are our mothers, they make us laugh and cry and love, and they always inspire us.

Run Like the Wind

By Maryann Macdonald and Ann Ingalls

Mom,

You were a speed demon on the road of life. At six, you were such a fast runner that you won first place in a competition among your peers at Euclid Beach in Cleveland. You so outdistanced the other runners that they pitted you against the seven-year-olds. You beat all of them, as well as the eight-, nine-, and ten-year-olds, after which you were retired from the contest.

At age seven, you were also picking up fees for your mother's employment agency clients. You could be counted on to run straight to the bank with the money. By high school, your fast feet made you a valued basketball player. Not only were you captain of the girls' team, but also you were the only girl on the boys' team. One of your proudest moments was the time you scored forty points in a single half to lead a victory against all-male rivals.

During World War II you worked in a chemical plant. When acid splashed on your face, your quick reaction kept you from losing your pale Irish complexion. As the sole female chemist employed by the plant, you parked your bicycle among all the men's cars. This caught our father's eye, and he won your heart by taking you to a basketball game.

As children, we could count on you pushing us on the swings as high as they would go and taking us on the merry-go-round at breakneck speed. Once the family could afford a station wagon, you demonstrated your legendary lead foot every Sunday, racing our neighbors home from eight o'clock Mass. In your zeal to win one Sunday, however, you blew up the transmission. Dad just laughed, calling you "my wild Irish rose."

You expected good things from life and liked to have fun. Fortunately, you made sure we took a family vacation every year in that station wagon. Unfortunately, the car was always packed with ten people, a week's bedding, clothes, and the ever-present diaper pail.

Your one vanity was shoes—gorgeous spike heels, red alligator with open toes, and black velvet heels with swirls of rhinestones. Unfortunately, when it came to children's shoes, you thought orthopedic. The first thing you did every morning was shine all our shoes and line them up on the kitchen counter behind our lunch bags.

You always pin curled your hair in the afternoons, and fluffed it up before Dad came home, applying lipstick to your lips and cheeks. This effect was offset by the fact that you tied your hair back with a shoelace. But you did have a taste for glamour, and when you went out on Saturday nights with Dad in your Persian lamb coat, you always trailed the scent of Shalimar.

Raised during the Depression, you were a thrift queen, making treasure hunts out of every garage sale. When given bear meat by a Michigan hunter one year, you ground it up and made it into spaghetti sauce that seemingly lasted forever. Another economy was home haircutting. Fortunately, you stopped cutting our hair yourself when we went to high school. Unfortunately, you favored the "Dollar-a-Do" barber.

Everyone was welcome at our house. You taught us to share whatever we had with whoever showed up. Lucky for us, you made a great roast beef dinner with mashed potatoes. On the flip side, however, you loved liver and squash and thought everyone else should learn to love them too!

When you had only four kids left at home, you needed a new challenge, so you returned to hairstyling, this time for residents of a home for the elderly run by the Little Sisters of the Poor. You did this for twenty-five years.

Those of us who shared the road of life with you knew that you didn't give up easily. Your motto was "keep going," and you did, even after your cerebral hemorrhage in 1991. According to doctors, your survival was a miracle, but it came with a price. The biggest challenge of your life was living in the slow lane. Despite that, those who cared for you always commented on the fact that you never complained.

Through it all you continued to share your wisdom with your children: "Pick your battles." "Don't examine things too closely." "Keep it simple—don't overdo." You enjoyed a good story and had a quick laugh until the very end.

Everyone who visited us in our home will always remember how you said good-bye. You would give the biggest hug ever and then stand, waving good-bye again and again, blowing kisses until at last we were out of sight.

Just in case you're doing that now, Mom, we're waving back.

WITH LOVE AND ADMIRATION,

Maryann and Ann
Dearborn, Michigan

Maryann Macdonald grew up in a large family in Michigan. Author of twenty-one children's books, she is based in New York City, works in the Authors in the Schools program, and serves as UN liaison for the International Board on Books for Young People.

Ann Ingalls, the fourth of her mother Winnie's eight children, has worked as a teacher in elementary and special education for over thirty years. Just like her mother, Ann loves children.

Fly Away Home

BY ARJEAN COLLINS SPAITE

Dear Mom,

I have so many wonderful memories of my childhood, raised in a house filled with love and laughter, by parents who were, and always would be, there for us no matter what the circumstance. You always encouraged my older brothers and me to try new things, and to be the best that we could be at all endeavors. That was not necessarily an easy lesson for a shy, timid girl like me, but fortunately I had your example to follow.

Just prior to my twelfth birthday, you and Dad went on a two-week vacation to Hawaii. I remember it clearly because it was the first vacation I could ever recall you two taking without any children. Both you and Dad had sacrificed many of your own worldly desires over the years, and now you were finally getting a vacation in paradise.

With your children safely deposited at Grandma's, you embarked on a grand adventure. It was the first time in your life that you'd set foot on an airplane, and it would be taking you far from the gentle, rolling hills of Ohio, across mountains and an ocean. Years later, you confessed to me how nervous you were about flying, but at the time, you looked cool and calm as a morning mist.

But you weren't taking any chances. Around your neck you wore a chain, and on that chain was a Christian cross, a Catholic crucifix, a Star of David, and even a Buddha! Despite being raised Methodist you were going to cover all bases, just in case something went horribly wrong on the way to paradise.

As the plane took off you said a little prayer to any and all gods who were there to listen: *I've never been to Hawaii. Please, God, if the plane has to crash, let it crash on the way back, so that I at least get my vacation first.*

It was a funny and quirky experience to think of now, and it still brings a smile to my face as I retell it, but it was a lesson from you that I took to heart. As this timid girl grew older, and opportunities to try new things came my way, I often remembered your first flight. I'd put on my imaginary chain, bearing so many different symbols, and say a little prayer to please let everything go all right, and if it didn't, at least let things come crashing down after I had the experience.

Those little prayers followed me to college, through marriage, childbirth, a return to college, karate classes, a new career, my CPA exam, and many other countless endeavors. I think of you, Mom, every time I get onto a plane, and I remember your words each time I stand back and let my children experience life on their own. Your words and actions are the talisman that sees me through each new and different life experience.

From you I learned that if you aren't willing to try, you can never achieve anything. Sitting safely at home means you won't be on a plane that crashes, but you'll never see the beauty of a sunset over the ocean, or walk along a sandy beach. If you don't apply for the job, you'll never get rejected, but you'll never feel the joy of being hired and having your merits appreciated. If you don't write the story that is in your heart, it will never be read.

So today, Mom, I write this letter of love. I thank you for giving me this gift—the willingness and courage to do anything in life. I hope I have passed your lessons on to my boys, and that they'll put on their imaginary chains—hung with every symbol they need—and sail off with a prayer that if they fail, may they at least have the experience first.

ALL MY LOVE,

Arjean
Boardman, Ohio

Arjean Collins Spaite is a CPA who resides in Boardman, Ohio, with her husband, three mostly grown sons, and two dogs. She's a black belt in karate who enjoys reading and writing in her spare time.

The World Is Your Oyster

By Tashina Sydney Knight

Dear Mom,

You have always told me that I am unique. Sometimes that was a good thing, like when my painting made it onto the front cover of our local newspaper. Sometimes, not so good, like when I was eighteen and you offered to pay for a whole new wardrobe for me if I would just wear something—anything—other than black.

What I didn't know at age eighteen was that you were the support and strength that allowed me the freedom to explore my uniqueness. Looking back, I see that all along you've taught me that I can be whoever I most want to be. All I have to do is try.

There's a story that you told me when I was about twelve years old that had great impact on my life. It started when you applied for a secretarial job in an insurance company. You wanted a better job, and you knew you needed to get your foot in the door somewhere, but there weren't many jobs in the insurance industry open to women in the 1950s. After handing in your application at your interview, you were given instructions to go to a room and join others so that you could take a test. You assumed that this would be a typing test, but when you got to the room you were surprised to find only tables and chairs—and a room filled with men.

It seemed a little strange, but since most people had already started the test, you took the paper and sat down. After completing the test, you waited in a courtyard for the scoring to be completed. While in conversation with one of the other men from the room, you learned that you'd just taken the entry-level management test.

You could've told them that you'd taken the test by mistake and that you had meant to apply for a different job, but the greatest lesson I've learned from you is that when an opportunity arises, grab it with both hands and don't let go. When you were called back into the room, you were told that you had the highest score. As a result, you went on to become one of the top insurance executives in the state of California, and no one ever suggested that you didn't belong there.

Still, after all your business success, it was your dream to show your creative side to the world. So, after more than thirty-five years in the insurance industry, you left to conquer the world of creating and selling jewelry. I watched you struggle at first, hands cramping from bending silver wire to make countless pairs of earrings, and burning your fingers working hot glass in a kiln. But despite that, there was never any doubt in my mind that you wouldn't succeed, because you've always possessed a strong drive to show the world that you can go as far as your dreams will take you.

You make spectacular jewelry and have made a good life for yourself, but what means more to me is how you make customers who shop with you feel good about themselves. You always take the time to show people how they too can make something creative that they can feel proud of.

I write this letter to honor you, Mom. I don't think you realize what a big inspiration you've been in my life.

LOVE,

Tashina
Austin, Texas

Tashina Sydney Knight is a mixed-media artist living in Austin with her husband. She is an avid reader and amateur meteorologist who endeavors to live her life with the exuberance of her mother.

The Broccoli Queen

By Dianna Graveman

Dear Mom,

It was a typical Saturday, which meant grocery-shopping day at our house: my least-favorite chore. On that particular day, I set out under cloudy skies to maneuver my car through crowded lanes of weekend traffic, knowing when I arrived at the store I'd have to negotiate a maze of aisles jammed with shoppers and their overflowing carts.

My gloomy morning disposition during that particular foray was not solely due to my distaste for grocery shopping. Earlier in the morning mail I'd received another rejection—a "thanks, but no thanks" letter—from a company where I'd applied for a teaching position. I was beginning to think that leaving my secure but unfulfilling job to pursue something more desirable was a risk I shouldn't have taken. My husband had tried to make a joke about having a midlife crisis in an effort to cheer me up, but I couldn't see the humor. There's nothing funny about trying to change careers at age forty-nine.

Once inside the dreaded store, I pushed my cart toward the produce aisle, my grouchy demeanor in full swing. The "I'm cranky" time bomb I was carrying must have been ticking loudly, because it seemed my fellow shoppers took one glance at me and discreetly shifted their attention to the potatoes or onions, rather than hazard a chance at sharing my space by the broccoli bin. It was then that I felt someone's eyes on me.

Who dares challenge me when I'm buying my greens?

I looked to my left and my right, but everyone was out of bomb-blast range. Then I looked at the broccoli laid out before me like soldiers in formation. I looked up.

Secured to the rim of the shelf hanging over the broccoli was a photograph of a woman with a wide grin. She was holding two stalks of broccoli on top of her head, the bushy shoots sticking out from her coifed hair like a bizarre set of antennae. She looked like *My Favorite Martian's* mother. But she wasn't. She was my mother. I stared at your photo in disbelief, Mom. There you were, smiling proudly, despite the fact that a pair of vegetative antennae appeared to be sprouting from your head.

Upon arriving home, I immediately called you, remembering that a few years before you had won a prize at that store for submitting a tip on how to keep vegetables fresh. You were one of the winners of the first round in that contest, but there was a bigger prize to be won—$100 worth of free groceries. In order to be eligible, you had to have your photograph taken to be displayed along with your award-winning food tip.

"Oh, no," you said when I told you about the picture at the grocery store. "Tell me they don't have that silly picture hanging up somewhere!"

The truth is none of us could figure out why they asked you to hold broccoli on your head for that picture. As I roamed the produce aisle after realizing you had broccoli-queen status, I noticed that yours wasn't the only bit of food sensationalism. One of the other contestants juggled cantaloupe, while another cradled a zucchini like a baby. Evidently, the store's public relations department has a strange sense of humor.

Regardless of the inevitable photographic evidence, Mom, you kept your eye on the prize and did what they asked, even though you were a little concerned about what people might think. You took the risk of looking silly for a chance at the big prize, and when we laughed at that picture, you laughed too.

Until I saw your photo that day, I'd forgotten about that contest, and somewhere along the way I'd also forgotten it's sometimes okay, and even necessary, to take a risk. Most importantly, it's *really* okay to laugh at yourself when things don't go according to plan. These are just a few of the things you've taught me many times over the years, Mom, but it took your grocery-store photograph—the one I've affectionately dubbed *My Favorite Mother*—to remind me again.

Thanks for the tip, Mom.

LOVE,

Dianna

St. Charles, Missouri

Dianna Graveman is a short-story writer and college instructor. Her nonfiction and fiction works have been published in several national publications. She lives with her husband and children in Missouri.

A Thoroughly
Modern Mother

BY STELLA WARD WHITLOCK

Dear Mother,

Though born in 1903, you were a thoroughly modern
woman. In many ways, you were way ahead of your
time—an independent thinker, a working professional
with a successful career, a leader in your church and
community, and a deeply committed parent and family
caregiver. What's even more important is that you
encouraged me to be just as independent and involved.
Your often repeated advice was "Whatever you want to
do, you can do it! Just do your best."

I can never thank you enough for all you did for me
and taught me through your words and your actions
during your ninety-nine years here on earth. From you,
Mother, I learned the value of an education. You attended Florida State University at a time when a college degree was not considered important for women—and you
certainly didn't waste that education. Before your marriage, you owned and operated your own kindergarten.
Then you had a second career as a reporter and women's
editor for the *Tampa Tribune.* You interviewed the
famous people of your day, including Admiral Richard
Byrd. You flew across Tampa Bay in a one-engine bi-
plane, and traveled across the United States by train.

You were active in your community as well. As a teenager, you delivered meals to families quarantined by the terrible flu epidemic of 1918, cooking big pots of soup and carrying them around the neighborhood. Following quarantine guidelines, you knocked on doors, left food on doorsteps, and watched from the curb to see that someone in the house was well enough to retrieve it. As an adult, you broadcast your own weekly radio show for several years, and you worked in service organizations such as the Tampa Woman's Club and the Daughters of the American Revolution.

True to your ideas about the importance of education, you stayed involved at the various schools I attended. Somehow you made time to serve as room-mother for my elementary-school classes. You baked hundreds of cookies and cupcakes for school functions, chaperoned field trips and school dances, volunteered to read stories and tutor in the classroom, served as PTA president, and planned carnivals and fundraisers. In spite of our limited income, you managed our family resources so well that I was able to enjoy such experiences as the Little Theatre, the Tampa Symphony, piano lessons, church camps and conferences, and Girl Scouts.

You didn't neglect spirituality, either. Our family never ate a meal without first giving thanks, and we never went to bed without saying our prayers. In church, you led the Women's Circles, taught Sunday school and Bible school, served as president of the Women of the Church, greeted newcomers, and often carried food and flowers to the sick, elderly, and shut-ins. You were also an adviser to youth groups and sang in the church choir. Unfortunately, try as I might, I didn't inherit your musical ability. To this day I sing off-key. Thanks to your sacrifices to give me piano lessons, however, I can play hymns for congregational singing.

Later in life, after my sister and I left the nest, you became a caregiver again. You cared for my grandmother, whose failing memory and physical limitations required constant attention. Later, you nursed my father, who suffered from diabetes, severe asthma, and heart disease. You tended his needs as he endured amputations of both legs, colon cancer, two heart attacks, and a series of strokes.

By your example, Mother, you taught me the importance of independence and service to others. You were a leader in every aspect of life. Your spirit of adventure, your self-sufficiency, and your abiding concern for others have been a constant inspiration.

Thank you for loving me; taking care of me; and teaching, encouraging, and inspiring me. I love you.

YOUR DAUGHTER,

Stella Lois
Fayetteville, North Carolina

Stella Ward Whitlock is a writer, wife of a Presbyterian minister, mother of four adult children, and grandmother of seven. Both her daughters have the middle name Lois in honor of their grandmother.

Portrait of a Mother

BY WILLIAM CASSIUS DIVNEY

Dear Mom,

When I paint a portrait of you in my mind, it could rival the famous women of historical literature and art. Beautifully posed, with that trademark twinkle in your eye and your infectious laughter, the world should see you as I do. The words of advice you have whispered in my ear stay with me, forever part of my conscience.

Throughout my youth, you were instrumental in making me a gentleman. You brought me solace in my darkest hours and taught me how to accept people by keeping an open mind. You were always emotionally available and never made me feel ashamed for expressing my feelings. You gave me the tools to learn boundaries, and taught me to put my own agenda behind me when others needed support, and to always listen to others.

Mom, I can't tell you how much that built up my character. The ability to see the bigger picture, to observe my surroundings, to be a team player—all of these lessons helped me foster lifelong friendships, garner respect from others, and instill leadership qualities that are part of me to this day. Under the most stressful circumstances I'm able to take a step back, let my emotions flow, pick myself up, and take charge. It took me quite a few years to incorporate these virtues into my day-to-day life, but with your guidance I've finally accomplished this.

When I was a child, you helped me conquer my dyslexia by rewarding me with a book whenever I cleaned my room. First there was the *Grease* film book, followed by a series of books about morals and values. I hope you don't regret allowing me to read *Watership Down* after I woke up one night screaming that there was a rabbit lodged inside my throat! My enthusiasm for reading grew stronger, and at age seventeen I found myself in an advanced English class in high school.

Your courage, independence, and creativity are more traits that you have passed down to me, Mom. Your ability to find humor and beauty in the simple things is one of your shining attributes. You carry that same zest whether shopping for antiques, decorating the house, or dancing to a Donna Summer song in the middle of the living room. You never take life for granted, and that has made you a successful wife, mother, artist, and businesswoman.

After years of selling art, working as a social worker, and raising two children, you plunged into the dog-eat-dog world of mortgage financing. You quickly flourished and became one of the top mortgage originators in the country. That isn't surprising, considering that you're one of the most dependable and responsible people I know. Whether it was rescuing the family cat from the roof in the middle of the night or helping me when I struggled with math homework, you were always there. Your spontaneity and knack for poking fun certainly got the best of me when I was nine years old. You managed to convince me that I could take an egg out of the refrigerator and hatch it. I fell for that fib, hook, line, and sinker, and hovered over the egg three hours a night for an entire week. While a chick never emerged, you certainly exposed how naive I could be, and gave everyone in the house a good laugh. Whenever people call me crazy in a fun-loving way I often think of you, Mom. In fact, if people actually thought that I *was* crazy I would point my finger at you. Always cunning and witty, your eccentricity never ceases to amaze me.

As I make my way through life, through the good times and bad, I can still smell the fresh paint on your canvases. You brought flowers to life with your intensity and passion for detail. I bring the same intensity to my own interests and endeavors and I feel enriched knowing that I was schooled by a pro—you.

With every stroke of your paintbrush, you've brought depth of perception and color to my life. For that I salute you, Mom.

LOVE ETERNAL,
YOUR SON,

Cassius
New York, New York

William Cassius Divney holds theatre arts and public relations degrees from Boston University. A graduate student at Columbia University, he's a director, actor, and animal activist. He dedicates this letter to his grandmother, Sara Staller-Divney.

Sixty-Five Nights of Sleep

By Parise Zeleny

I love you, Mom.

I miss you when I am at school. Mommy, I like it when you kiss me. I like helping make pancakes with you in the mornings. I like eating them with you, too. I like helping you make cookies for desserts. I like to cuddle with you at night in bed.

If I could give you a present, I would give you 65 nights when you could sleep in. I would give you a horse to go horse-riding on. I would give you a black poodle.

You make me feel happy. I want to give you a kiss.

LOVE,

Monterey Peninsula,
California

Parise Zeleny is a four-year-old preschooler who loves to dictate letters to friends and family, as long as someone is willing to listen and transcribe. Once she can write for herself, there will be no stopping her, and the world will be flooded with missives.

The Glasgow Fiasco

BY DANIELLE GIARDINO MUTARELLI

Dear Mom,

I anxiously awaited your arrival in London, and the trip
we planned together to Scotland. I wanted desperately
to show you a good time, but I was at a complete loss as
to how to pull it off, being that I was accustomed to
budget travel. Somehow I couldn't envision you, my
stylish mother, sleeping on a train using a balled-up
sweatshirt as a pillow, or thinking that a crusty
baguette stuffed with sliced processed cheese, and a box
of wine constituted a decent meal. I couldn't imagine
you'd come all this way to experience the numerous
pitfalls that shoestring travel entailed. Yet you'd waited
so long to come here that I couldn't let you down.
Everything would have to be perfect.

As we left London and headed to Edinburgh, I was
most worried about accommodations. I always knew
you to be easygoing, but I gathered you drew the line at
sleeping in a youth hostel bunkbed with a room full of
strangers. Through a travel agent at the train station we
found a bed and breakfast, and the room was a dream. It
was newly decorated and immaculately clean; you
couldn't ask for a better place to stay. This was the kind
of experience you deserved.

We spent two beautiful days touring Edinburgh and the surrounding area. Everything about the trip thus far was smooth and perfect, so I wondered if all my worry was for naught. But in Glasgow, the weather turned, and so did our luck.

Given the success we had with the train station travel agent in Edinburgh, we repeated the process in Glasgow. This time it was an exercise in futility, as we got lost, museums were closed, and it began to rain. Because of the weather, we didn't venture to our hotel until late in the evening—and that was a big mistake.

The hotel was called St. Enoch's, but for all your Catholic education you could not recall who St. Enoch was. We entered our room, attempting to ignore its many flaws, and its pungent aroma of Chinese takeout. "Maybe it'll seem better after a shower," you said optimistically.

I sat dejectedly on the lumpy bed. This room was my worst fear. It wasn't worth half of what we'd paid. We'd gotten royally ripped off, and it was my fault. Glasgow was officially a disaster.

You emerged from the bathroom toweling off your hair, pausing to examine the towel. "What did you get on this?" you asked, pointing at a black streak on the towel.

"Mom, I didn't touch that towel."

You shrieked and threw it across the room.

After the shock wore off, you started laughing, and I joined you. Once we started, we couldn't stop. The room suddenly became hilarious. We opened the curtains to reveal a scenic brick wall. We tried to think of alternate uses for the hideous bedspread, deciding it could be a loofah because when I rubbed it against my arm it actually removed several layers of skin. You also thought it would make excellent military camouflage since no one with a set of eyes could bear to look at it.

We then discovered that there was only a half-used roll of toilet paper in the bathroom, and eyed with horror—through snorts and guffaws—the cleanliness of the sheets. You picked up the limp pillows from the bed and draped them across your arms. As you stood there with outstretched arms you said, "I think I figured out who St. Enoch was. He was the patron saint of bad accommodations, and this is what he looked like."

I fell off the bed laughing.

As I looked up at you, clutching your sides, your face streaked with tears, it occurred to me that this was going to be the highlight of our trip. You turned misfortune into fortune.

Years later we still talk about the time we spent in Edinburgh, but it is the Glasgow fiasco that makes us laugh. In that hotel room you showed me that any bad situation can be turned around, and that's a lesson that has carried me through much more difficult situations in my life.

There are times that I struggle to see the lightness of certain events, but you've always been a phone call away. And with those calls I know that my worries will soon subside and that laughter is imminent. You taught me that life is imperfect, but that a good sense of humor will always be my best defense.

Thank you, Mom.

LOVE,

Dani

Merrimack, New Hampshire

Danielle Giardino Mutarelli is an aspiring young writer who divides her writing time between fiction and nonfiction, loving both equally. She lives in New Hampshire with her husband and their four-year-old son.

Survival of the Fittest

By Hana Kim

Dear Mom,

When you had your first seizure, we were both devastated. You'd never had any health problems before, and you thought you were in great shape. When the doctor in the emergency room suggested it was a stroke, we were stunned. Later, the neurologist wanted to speak to me by myself, and I knew it was bad news. He said the words "brain tumor," and all the strength went out of my legs.

You had a brain tumor, and the doctors didn't know why. They even had a fancy name for your tumor: meningioma. Both the neurologist and the neurosurgeon said it was most likely a benign tumor, but that you needed an operation to remove it.

I know that you debated whether to have the surgery. It was a serious procedure, and the doctors gave us a long list of possible risks, including stroke, heart attack, and even death. You worried what would happen if you did survive the surgery, as the tumor pressed against the area of your brain that controlled speech and memory. If they removed the tumor, would you be able to speak? Would you recognize my face when you awoke?

You debated, but ultimately decided to have the surgery. You wanted that tumor out of your head. You tried to stay strong in the months before the surgery, keeping worry to yourself, but we were both scared and nervous. During the drive to the hospital on the day of your operation, we were both very quiet. You cried once, but tried to hide your tears.

I almost cried when the surgical resident shaved one side of your head, but you remained strong and brave the entire time. Five hours later, your operation was over, but it was several more hours until I could see you. Each minute felt like an eternity.

When they wheeled you into the Intensive Care Unit, a nurse came out and said you were looking for me. When I entered the room I was shocked that you were awake and alert, and that you turned your head toward me and waved. You recognized me.

I was so relieved that I was speechless. Then you spoke my name, and I knew everything was going to be okay. Your recovery went so well that even the nurses were amazed. Four days after the operation, you insisted on leaving the hospital without a wheelchair, and you walked out the door, your stride brisk and strong. No one would have guessed that you'd just had brain surgery.

Since then you've taken even stronger steps. You completely changed your lifestyle by eating healthy food and exercising more. You managed to lose the excess fifteen pounds that had been bothering you for so long. You are stronger and healthier now than you were a decade ago.

Thank you, Mom, for surviving brain surgery. On May 13, 2006, it will have been three years since the operation that removed the tumor on your brain. I want to thank you for being so strong throughout the entire ordeal. You beat the tumor, and I know that you can beat any other obstacle that comes your way.

I am so proud to say that you are my mom. You are the strongest person I have ever known, and every day I hope and pray that you stay strong and healthy for the rest of a very long life. I love you.

LOVE,

Hana
Garden Grove, California

Hana Kim is a freelance writer in Garden Grove, California. She has published short fiction in several E-zines, and is currently working on a collection of short stories.

Countdown to Mommy

By Tessa Hudson

Dear Mom,

If I could put a percent on you, you would be 90% pure love and 10% of other wonderful things. You have been protecting me for 11 years, 6 months, 2 days, 11 hours, 40 minutes and 5 seconds. You are sweet and kind, most of all caring. I wouldn't have it any other way.

LOVE,

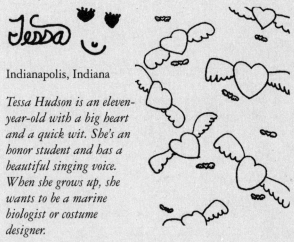

Indianapolis, Indiana

Tessa Hudson is an eleven-year-old with a big heart and a quick wit. She's an honor student and has a beautiful singing voice. When she grows up, she wants to be a marine biologist or costume designer.

The Mirror Has Two Faces

BY KATHY LYNN REED

Dear Mama,

It seemed like everyone was against you. The people at church took Daddy's side. Even your own father refused to speak to you. He just couldn't understand how a God-fearing woman in the sixties could walk out on her marriage of fifteen years. Everyone was so quick to judge, but they didn't know the whole story.

I remember the nights that you and Daddy argued until the wee hours while I covered my head with my blankets to drown out the loud voices. You always smiled for me and went about the day, doing what you needed to do to take care of me, but I saw your eyes when you thought no one was looking. I saw the deep sorrow and I heard your sighs. You were miserable, and you tried so hard to convince everyone—yourself included—that you were all right.

I watched from the window one rainy Saturday morning when the ladies from your office came to pick you up to go shopping. I saw you dry your tears before coming back inside after telling them Daddy said you "couldn't go and spend any money on foolish things." You came in each Friday with your paycheck in hand and gave it to Daddy. He would give you back what he thought was enough for the weekly groceries. Later, I would watch your embarrassment when you would come up short at the register when you paid for them. You couldn't write a check because your name wasn't even on the account.

I'm sure you spent many sleepless nights listing the reasons you should stay with him—the same reasons that would be thrown in your face later by those you thought cared about you. But you told me that you got up one morning and looked at yourself in the mirror. You took a good, hard look, and finally made the decision that your happiness meant something. You told him you were leaving, and you took me and left. I watched Daddy's face as we drove away. I guess I expected him to cry, but all I saw was anger. I was glad we were leaving.

After that day, you became another person. You laughed and joked and danced. You had friends over for visits. You fell in love again. You began to live.

Years later, I found myself in the same type of situation with a man who could've been my father's double. My self-esteem was practically nonexistent, and I'd stopped laughing and smiling and singing. Everyone told me I had to stay with him because I had nowhere to go, but I looked at myself in the mirror one morning after twenty years of marriage and made the same decision you did. I left. I worked two jobs, finished my degree, and I survived.

If not for you I'd still be in an unhappy marriage. If not for your example, I'd have never found the courage to get out. You taught me so many valuable lessons through the things you said, but your actions spoke the loudest. Because of you, I learned to live.

Thanks, Mom.

LOVE,

Kathy
Decatur, Alabama

Kathy Lynn Reed is a mother of four, a former teacher, and a full-time writer who lives in Decatur, Alabama, with her husband and two doggies. She has published several short stories. Her Web site is at www.writingsbykathy.com.

Firm Foundations

BY AMY AMMONS MULLIS

Dear Mom,

Many times you can look back on your life and recall those moments a mother and daughter share when each one comes away knowing that life is good and special and sweet. Times when you have the unshakable feeling that your life fits just right. I can't help thinking of the girdle incident as one of those moments.

Remember the day we went girdle shopping? You stood in front of the mirror with eight ounces of cross-your-knees latex clinging to your legs while I stood and watched like a three-toed sloth at a ballroom dance class.

It all started because four decades of biscuits and gravy had sandbagged your midsection so it threatened to overflow its boundaries like strained peas down a baby's chin. You were at the point where, physically speaking, life was more like a bowl of Jell-O than a bowl of cherries. As a result, your relationship with wardrobe was like my relationship with long division—it was something that had to be dealt with, but it never worked out quite right. There was always something left over that didn't fit in.

On that shopping day, we waddled downtown in search of foundation garments suitable for camouflage purposes. One of our earliest forays was to a well-to-do department store that smelled of polished wood and old money—a store that kept evening gloves in a glass case, and people actually bought them! I'll never forget that saleslady. She was tall and thin, spoke in third-person vague, and her eyes swept over us like Lemon Pledge over dust bunnies. With a little effort and six months of Dale Carnegie classes, she might have developed the friendly appeal of a hemorrhoidal wolverine.

Loaded down with enough industrial-strength elastic to stabilize the women's World Cup soccer team, we staggered into a carpeted dressing room. I know now that restrictive foundation garments should come with a warning label from the surgeon general. The first taste of flesh sent that girdle into an elastic feeding frenzy. It snapped around your knees like a Burmese python after two weeks on a grapefruit diet, the waistband popped up around your arm like a runaway window shade, and the tummy control panel ate the freckles off your arms.

"Cut it off," you wheezed, giggling as you struggled to free yourself from the clutches of the maniacal garment.

In my mind I could picture us having to pay for that monstrosity and calling Dad from the emergency room to see if our insurance covered girdle removal by a Harvard Med School graduate.

"No way," I thought to myself, "we'll have to pay full price." I turned to you. "Grab the doorknob. I'll brace against you with my foot and pull."

Just then, the perky tap-tap of high heels sounded outside the door. Stretching back from the doorknob like spitballs in a slingshot, we watched in horror as the door opened. From that point on, everything happened really fast, and that girdle disappeared quicker than a teenage boy on take-out-the-trash day. The salesgirl—all padded bra and press-on nails—peered in to find us in a sweaty, panting pile, wiping tears from our eyes as we laughed. I think you still had the imprint of a floral design on your thigh. She raised a meticulously penciled eyebrow.

"Can I get you anything?"

You eyed the lurking piles of unopened boxes. "How about the jaws of life?" you said.

These days when I'm discouraged and worried that, despite my best efforts, my middle will overlap my sides, I remember an afternoon when we ran giggling from a high-dollar department store to a corner drugstore soda fountain and shared a Coke and a banana split. We learned an important lesson that day: it's better to stand on firm foundations than wear them.

LOVE,

Amy Doodle
Greer, South Carolina

Amy Ammons Mullis is from a niblet-sized town in South Carolina where everyone knows what size everyone else wears. She counts the memories of her mom among her firmest foundations.

Fifty and Fabulous

BY PAULA MUNIER

Dear Mom,

It's March 14, 2006, and on this, my fiftieth birthday in the middle of an all-too-predictable midlife crisis, I ask myself: Who am I? And more importantly, why have I failed to become the perfect woman my mother is, and has always been—unfailingly—every day of my life?

Of course, you gave me life, but that's the least of it. What you really gave me was a model of being in the world, more specifically, a model of being a woman in the world.

I used to think that my failure to live up to this model was inevitable, simply a matter of generational differences. You are a Lady with a capital "L." Coming of age in the fifties, you personify the grand ladies of your era. As regal and willowy as Grace Kelly, as discreet and diplomatic as Jackie Kennedy, as chic and compassionate as Audrey Hepburn, you embody all the qualities that defined femininity at that time.

It was a definition that would come under attack while you were still a young woman. You and Gloria Steinem are the same age—a fact that always somehow startles me, as you appear to stand at opposite poles of the female spectrum.

But appearances can be deceiving.

While some of your contemporaries were protesting the Vietnam War, experimenting with drugs and free love, and marching for women's rights, you were the quintessential colonel's wife, pouring tea, playing bridge, and praying for your husband's safe return from a conflict you fully supported. (At least I assume you supported it. But as I realized at sixteen when I found *The Sensuous Woman* by "J" hidden under the family photos in the hope chest, there's always been more to you than I knew. You keep yourself to yourself—another lesson I have yet to learn.)

Yet you were surprisingly independent as well. While Dad was off soldiering, you were moving our household from country to country with aplomb, working part-time bookkeeping jobs when you could, and driving that big Buick Riviera all over Europe by yourself so that your only child could see Paris, Amsterdam, London, and more.

Unlike other women of your generation, you resented neither the strictures society placed on you as a woman, nor the sacrifices you made for husband, children, and country. You could've been a great artist, but you happily settled for decorating your many homes and those of your friends and family. You could have stayed close to home back in Indiana after Dad retired, but instead you headed west to be close to me. You could have spent your golden years playing golf with your peers, but you spent them playing Crazy Eights with your grandchildren. Now, with me in New

England and the kids mostly grown and scattered from Los Angeles to Lausanne, you've made your desert home in suburban Las Vegas the one place on earth where we all feel safe, secure, and loved.

There are many lessons I should have learned from you that I have not. I never learned that: (1) discretion is the better part of valor; (2) if you can't say anything nice, don't say anything at all; or (3) if you want to get someone's attention, whisper.

Where you are patient, soft spoken, and calm, I am short-tempered, foul-mouthed, and high-strung. Where you are impeccably dressed, impossibly thin, and impenetrably self-possessed, I am curvy, frenetic, and running my pantyhose as we speak. I will never be as tall or thin or chic as you are. I will never be happily married for more than fifty years, as you are. (Even if I were to marry a man worth keeping fifty years today and lived to be 100, we both know that I tend to choke around the tenth wedding anniversary.) I will never be as good with people—or as smart about them—as you are.

You'll read this and say, as you invariably do, "This is not true. You are ten times the woman I am. Look at all that you've accomplished, the three beautiful children you've raised, the obstacles you've overcome, and you've done it all by yourself, without help from anyone. You are amazing!"

Which leads us to the most important lesson of all, the one even I managed to learn, thanks to you. Mothers don't need to be perfect, they just need to love with a perfectly open heart. In this critical respect, I am my mother's daughter, after all. I've not been as patient, kind, or well mannered a mother as you've been, but that's okay. My kids know I love them, because I show them, just as you have shown me. I tell them how amazing they are, just as you have told me. I am their biggest fan, just as you have been mine. When they walk into the room, my face lights up, just as your face does, just as every mother's face should. Writer Toni Morrison says that's the most important thing you can do for a child, but you already knew that. And I know that you're thinking, "Who needs a writer to tell you that?"

And of course you're right, Mom, as always. You don't need a writer to tell you that. All you need is my mother.

LOVE,

Paula

Pembroke, Massachusetts

A writer, editor, and novelist, Paula Munier owes everything she is—and is not—to her mother. Mother to Alexis, Gregory, and Mikey, she lives in rural Massachusetts in a lakeside cottage with her family, two dogs, and a cat.

2.

You Made Me Who I Am Today

I f you painted a picture that represented your mother, what would you paint? Would you swirl together all the colors of a rainbow? Show a gentle stream weaving through a forest glen? Depict a brilliant sun rising over a sparkling sea? Mothers color our world. They tint our minds with magical and effervescent tales that bring our perceptions into clear focus.

As we grow, we learn that the world is not black and white. Our mothers educate us in all disciplines of life and guide us with their faith, optimism, practicality, and humor. From them we learn the value of what it is to truly live, and as a result of their lessons we become better, more colorful individuals. And as we create our own families, our mothers' wisdom trickles down from one generation to the next, forming a legacy in its wake.

At times we might not understand why it is our mothers act or react the way they do. Only in our later years do we realize their methods and their determination to keep us safe and secure. Look at your mother and you will see a kaleidoscope, a colorful mix of time-honored wisdom, tradition, faith, and courage painted right before your eyes.

The Magic of Moms and Rain Fairies

By Robin Courtright

Dear Mom,

I miss you most on rainy days. I think it's because that's where you've done your best work in my life—the canvases of possibilities you've painted across my stormy days.

As best I can remember, it began when I was four or five. On dreary days when there was nothing else to do, you taught me to find rain fairies dancing inside the circles created by raindrops landing rhythmically on our patio. You described them in perfect detail. One wore a lace jacket, and another was clad in a tiny purple ballerina dress. They had names like Bell and Opal, and they each had tiny colorful wings that glittered with diamond dust. They rode into our yard on raindrops, to dance on our patio and wait for the sun to lead them back to heaven on a rainbow.

You challenged me to press my nose to the glass and peer through the window until I could see the beauty that was inevitably waiting to be uncovered in a distressing moment of reality. There's always something more to be found in the rain than what you see. That's been a wonderful lesson that has stayed with me through all the seasons of my life.

I'm a grandmother now, and you're a great-grandmother. Today, as the rain dances down from the heavens over Texas, and while you read the paper in California, you feel as close as the stories that bound us together in magical places almost a half-century ago. You may have conjured up the fairy tales of my childhood with the sole intention of calming my tantrums or to give me something to do, but you wove an intricate tapestry of lifelong lessons from rain fairies and rainbows.

You taught me that perception is 10 percent vision and 90 percent faith. It's your lesson of pressing one's nose to the glass until your perception changes that has allowed me to rise above my perceived limitations. I may have traded some of my dreams for less glorious paths—sometimes by design and sometimes by mistake—but don't we all?

I have no regrets.

What is important and meaningful and most inspiring in life will never been seen with the naked eye. Those things are only seen with the heart.

You showed me that what is contained in the heart is of far greater value than what is tangible in the world around me. You laid a framework for the faith that continues to define me today. I've never been afraid to fail, because I have never feared to try. Who knows what magic can be found when you allow yourself to dance with the rain fairies—even if you're the only one who sees them?

On dreary rainy afternoons, you painted with words, whimsical magical scenes across my dimmed and frustrated imagination, until I became captivated by the sheer wonder of things unseen.

I became a writer, blending words until they find colors of their own in fertile fields of sentences no one else has ever written. I was never able to establish dimension with pencils and paint, instead preferring the invisible canvas of thought and imagination.

And even there in the framework, I see you.

Do you remember that horrible argument we had when I was twenty and proclaimed loudly that I never wanted to be like you? Thirty years have passed, and now I see that we all become so much like our mothers. There's no one better to be, really. Superheroes and white knights tend to lose their luster when tried by the fires of time, but mothers never do. There's a difference between illusion and true magic. Illusions fade to fables, but true magic is the stuff of rain fairies and mothers. Their magic is eternal; it lives within us and beyond us, a gift in hand and heart. Thank you for passing it on to me.

The rain has stopped outside my window, but not my thoughts of gratitude for who you've helped me become. I want to say that to you today. I would have liked to kiss your cheek, and hugged you too. Press your nose to the glass, Mom. Can you feel the magic?

I LOVE YOU AND MISS YOU,

Robin

Arlington, Texas

Robin Courtright is mother to two beautiful young women. A grandmother and freelance writer, she enjoys using her spare time to write devotional and inspirational material for children.

Silver Linings

BY RICK SUTHERLAND

Dear Mom,

Optimism and faith. Such simple words, such simple concepts. Mom, you personified those words. Even through many years of pain and debilitating physical degeneration, you manifested these ideals in every aspect of your life, and your relentless optimism has affected everyone you touched during your lifetime. It's only recently that I've come to realize that such an agreeable and positive outlook can take an incredible amount of work.

You were always the working mother, but I remember your being forced into an early retirement from a career that you thoroughly enjoyed; forced by a cruel and untreatable spinal deterioration. Seemingly unfazed, you launched into tending your home with Dad. You filled room after room with the most incredible displays of indoor horticulture. You sewed a closet-full of intricate outfits. You filled shelves with books on health and healing. You filled walls with lovely placards of cheerful sayings and inspirational thoughts.

As the years passed, the disease that took away your career also took away your ability to tend your lush indoor gardens. You replaced them with equally lush silk plantings that required less care, but you loved them no less. When sitting at the sewing machine became too painful, you knitted beautiful sweaters and scarves in the only recliner that could provide you some measure of comfort. Your library of health literature brought you little personal relief, but you made sure that Dad was filled with vitamins and minerals and the healthiest of diets, and he shows the benefits and vigor of your care to this day. Your placards of cheerful sayings and inspirational thoughts were no simple displays. You read them, you loved them, and most important, you lived them.

For all of those years, Mom, you never once complained of pain or uttered a sound that gave evidence of your discomfort. Ever cheerful, ever thoughtful, ever humorous, your spirit far surpassed anything any of us could see from the outside. It was almost too easy to forget just how difficult your trials had become, how debilitating and unkind your disease. And until very recently, it was far too easy to assume that your optimism and faith somehow came to you easily.

You know, Mom, that right now I'm in the midst of recovering from an auto accident that came within inches of being fatal, within fractions of an inch of causing paralysis. "It's a miracle you're alive," said the neurosurgeon after he'd viewed X-rays of my fractured neck. "Another miracle," he said, after determining that my extremities still functioned. You know that I know how lucky I am to have survived this; that I've counted my blessings and my loved ones every single day. You know that the months and the days and the hours and minutes that I was encased in a halo-vest restraint—a device that could have been designed in a medieval torture chamber—were the most difficult of my life. Throughout these past months, I've tried to let my dearest loved ones and wonderful friends know just how much I appreciate their kindness, their thoughtfulness, and their selfless help. And through these months, I've tried to be as optimistic and cheerful as I possibly could.

As I ponder this period in my life, I can't help but think of you. I have come to realize that the optimistic approach is not necessarily the easiest; that it can take some real work, a lot of soul-searching, and occasionally some out-and-out willpower to keep your eyes on the bright side.

You left this earth so many years ago, and this is a letter that can't be mailed, can't be opened, can't be read. But I know that you received this letter thought for thought and word for word as I wrote it. I know these things because of the gifts you gave me. For that, I am eternally grateful. It's because of you that I have that optimism, I have that faith.

ALL MY LOVE,

Rick

Depoe Bay, Oregon

Rick Sutherland has co-authored several books, and makes his home in the Pacific Northwest with his better half, Barb.

Laughter Is the Best Medicine

BY CHRIS GRANT

Dear Mama,

When I think back on my childhood, many of the things I treasure most about you are your incredible patience, easy-going nature, and your ability to laugh at adversity. I often wish I'd inherited these wonderful traits. Somehow they swam right past my side of the gene pool, and I ended up with a personality that is not calm, cool, or collected. Lucky for me, I have you! Whenever I have an anxious or stressful moment in my life, I can always count on you to make it easier. Your calm demeanor can instantly turn an upset and irrational daughter into a tranquil being.

Remember my first day of college? I was nervous about heading off to a big university where I knew no one. I was suddenly a very small fish in a great big pond. For a boost of confidence, I decided to "borrow" my older sister's new and beloved pair of Calvin Klein jeans to wear on my big day. Since I knew she'd never let me wear them, I pilfered them from her room and figured I'd have them back in her closet before she realized they were missing.

I anxiously drove to the university campus and quickly parked the car. Because I was nervous and running late, I didn't notice that the street I was crossing had just been freshly paved with tar. Being the klutz that I am, I tripped and fell hard onto the tar. When I got up, I realized I was encased in a gooey mess. My feet, hands, arms, shirt and, much to my horror, the Calvin Kleins were covered in tar.

Panic immediately set in. I knew I had to go home and change, so I ran back to my 1974 Pinto. I was already behind the wheel, when I realized I was sitting on—and now glued to—my cheap sheepskin seat covers.

As I was driving home I became increasingly upset. Not only was I missing my first college class, but your other daughter—my older and *much* bigger, stronger sister—was going to snap me in half like a twig when she realized what I'd done.

When I finally made it to our driveway I leaped from the car, failing to notice that the sheepskin from my seats had now attached itself in huge clumps to my tarred body. I burst through the front door and immediately ran to the phone to call you, and the phone cord became plastered to my arm. By the time you picked up the phone, I was sobbing, and I could tell by your voice that I'd scared you. By the way I was acting, I'm sure you thought I'd been in a car accident.

"Where are you? Are you okay? What's wrong?" you asked with motherly concern.

Through chokes and sputters, I finally managed to yell out, "I fell in tar!"

For a second, the phone went silent, but as I continued to relay my upsetting incident to you, I began hearing strange noises. Quieting my sobs for an instant, I listened closely, and then realized that all I could hear at the other end of the line was laughter. Not just giggles. Uncontrolled, roaring laughter. I know that you were thinking that this could only happen to "graceful Chrissy."

Being the caring Mom that you are, and knowing how upset I was, you immediately left work and came home to help me. As you entered through the front door, the look on your face said it all. Standing before you was your daughter, who looked like a sheep that had gone swimming in the La Brea Tar Pits.

Although you were trying hard to take the situation seriously, you took one look at me and started to laugh so hard that tears rolled down your face like a waterfall. And you know what? I started laughing, too. You took my distress and made me see the humor in it. You got me laughing at myself.

Thank you, Mama, for showing me how not to take life so seriously.

LOVE,

Chrissy
Wilsonville, Oregon

Chris Grant is a real estate appraiser in the Pacific Northwest, where she lives with her husband, Glen, and two cats, Bailey and Simba. To this day, she still hasn't replaced her sister's Calvin Kleins.

Body and Soul

BY ALEXANDRA PAJAK

Dear Mom,

You gave me the greatest gift a mother can give her daughter—an unconditional love of my body.

As I know you remember, the bookworm in me had little interest in television or beauty magazines as a teenager. Instead, my middle- and high-school days were filled with stories, poems, and diaries read and written beneath my bedroom covers by the light of my purple keychain flashlight—the one we bought at the gas station on one summer vacation we took.

Growing up in the South, I stuffed my summers with swimming, peach picking, Bible reading, and blackberry stealing from our neighbor's backyard. Did you know I stole those blackberries I offered to you for your morning Cheerios that one week? I hope you don't mind.

Despite my attempts at mind stretching and soul-searching, I didn't physically blossom until my late teens, but words you offered prevented me from ever feeling inadequate. My life as your daughter was not completely impenetrable from the piercing voices of those who proclaim the unreachable ideal of traditional beauty. The promise of the "perfection" of breasts and thighs, and hair and complexion, only available through surgery, squats and extensions, and face scrubs, still entered my world. This perfect world of lies and insults proclaimed itself most loudly on the magazine shelves of the grocery store, where large-busted women stared enticingly—taunting us—urging us to buy and compare and submit to their power.

When I turned twelve and boys turned into guys, I remember one day in the grocery store when we stood towering over the strawberry Fruit Roll-Ups and seven-grain bread loaves in our cart. You told me that advertising is full of deception, and that plastic surgery, digital enhancement, hair artists, and hours of makeup were cruel seductions and false promises. You pointed to a magazine cover featuring Cindy Crawford and said the words I'll never forget: "This isn't real. Look around you. No one really looks like this. Even Cindy Crawford herself doesn't wake up looking like Cindy Crawford. It's wrong for a woman to look at a magazine and say 'I want to look like that.' And it's wrong for a guy to say, 'I want a girlfriend who looks like that.' No one looks like that—not even the models themselves."

I don't know if your words were rehearsed and you had selected grocery shopping as the prime moment of such mother-daughter bonding, but I do know that our conversation was powerful. I have since shared your words with female friends of mine, but none of them has ever told me of a similar experience with their mother.

As a twenty-four-year-old living on my own, adult life can get a little lonely sometimes in between salaried hours, microwave meals, and city subways. I recently bought a television, and I'm amazed each day with the endless commercials for diet pills, and plastic surgery-related reality shows that pay no regard to the reality of a woman's beauty as it emerges through her soul, dreams, passions, and memories. I admit that while clutching my remote control and while pushing my own grocery cart at the store, I am sometimes seduced by the images. Am I too thin? Too small-breasted? Not fit enough? But those days are few.

As I live my days and nights and mornings and twilights, your words repeat themselves in my mind and in my heart, Mom. Your words—because they are yours—conquer every temptation, insult, and suggestion that my body is unattractive compared to the ideals of the media.

You gave me a gift, Mom—the gift of loving my body. I don't know how my body may curve and grow over the years or how our relationship may change over time, but I will always remember your message: You shall never compare yourself to other women. I hope my message to you is equally clear: No other mother compares to you.

Love,

Alexandra
Atlanta, Georgia

Alexandra Pajak has been published in several anthologies. She is a big fan of coffee, bears, good friends, and movies by the Coen brothers.

The Sweetest Mommy
BY CIERA HUDSON

To My Sweet Mother,

Mommy you are the sweetest mother. I wonder what Chcogo [Chicago] is like do you know mommy? I hope it is very cool Mommy you are as sweet as a flower you make us dinner that is also sweet

LOVE,

Indianapolis, Indiana

Ciera Hudson is seven years old and is a competitive gymnast. She always has a smile on her face and her mommy calls her "a little ray of sunshine." Ciera loves horses and drawing, and she wants to be a gymnastics teacher when she grows up.

Cyclone Sally

BY RANDY SCHUPPAN

Hey Mom,

"Wherever that man was, he drew a crowd." That's what they said about your dad, and I don't think the acorn fell far from the tree.

I have a copy of the high-school senior-class drama program where you played the lead in *Cyclone Sally*, and you've held that role throughout the stages of my life. In my mind, I catch glimpses of you as captain of the Bismarck, Missouri, girls' high school basketball team. I once asked your best friend, Ruby, "You played basketball on the team with Mom, didn't you?" I can still hear Ruby's answer: "Honey, nobody played basketball with your mother. We were only there to help her when she needed it."

What accounted for that magnetic aura about you? You were the youngest of five sisters, yet family events seemed to revolve around you. Your gravitational pull maintained closeness with all of our relatives. You were always searching for ways to hold the family in orbit and be there for those who needed advice and help. Not only your sons, but also your nieces and nephews came to you for a good portion of that.

I remember in my younger years when you took in laundry for other people, but I couldn't understand why. You seemed so energetic in your search for money. Once, most likely in an effort to keep me off the streets, you took me along on one of your home-products sales parties. Since we used those products in our home, I considered myself an authority on certain favorite items. I volunteered to the ladies my high opinion of the bath brush, because when it got wet it smelled like a dog! That wasn't pretty. Not only was I no help, but when you achieved your goal of getting your kids out of a rough neighborhood, I was the ingrate who said I didn't want to move.

It was always fun to be with you, Mom, but you could straighten the strings of your three boys faster than anyone I've ever known. A combination of that look and waggling your forefinger while steadily advancing in our direction made us quit. Whatever it was we were up to—we stopped.

When I was fifteen and learning to drive, my level of proficiency was considerably overblown by me. Traveling with me at the wheel, you commented once on something you felt I'd done wrong. I confidently let you know that I knew what I was doing, and offered you the opportunity to simply enjoy the ride. I was so puffed-up with my sense of maturity that, for the first time, I spoke to you as an equal. Subsequently, you told me to pull over. I made it to the curb, then turned to face you and the expected lecture.

I never even saw the left hook coming. What I did see were plenty of stars. No guy ever got a left hook past me like that. You were some athlete! You paused for effect, then waggled that finger at me and quietly said, "Don't you ever talk to me like that again." And I didn't. Ever.

You always loved it when I'd surprise you by coming home unexpectedly. I'd stop at a phone booth a few blocks away from the old homestead and dial your number. We'd casually chat, until you asked when I was coming home for a visit. Your reaction was always so much fun to hear when I'd say, "Oh, in about five minutes."

Once you even turned the tables on me, calling my college dorm to ask that I pick you up at the airport for a weekend visit. I didn't mention to you that I had a date and tickets to an important play at a theater downtown, so I decided to break the date and took you instead. This decision created a little havoc because the girl never went out with me again, and the play was a disaster. It had great reviews in the newspapers, but I'd known nothing at all about the plot when I bought the tickets. It was really raunchy, and I had to sit next to you through the whole thing. As we left the theater I couldn't think of anything to say, but you did. "I'm just glad you didn't take one of the college girls to see that," you ventured.

The youngest of five sisters, you were the first of them to pass on. You were always great company, Mom, and you left me with plenty to laugh about.

LOVE ALWAYS,

Randall
O'Fallon, Missouri

After forty-five years in science education, spanning the elementary grades through college, Randy Schuppan formed Ransch Productions to satisfy further interests in writing, storytelling, and photography.

A Window in Heaven

By Karen Noblitt

Dear Mama,

This letter is long overdue. Several times I have tried to transfer the words from my heart to paper, but I always felt I'd come up short. As the sixth anniversary of the day you left rapidly approaches, I figure that the time has finally come. I simply must express to you how I truly feel.

Do you know what I remember most about you? The way your presence could always calm me. The soft, cool feel of your touch as you stroked my hair before bedtime, and your beautiful voice singing softly in the kitchen as you washed dishes. Even though I am now grown, I still wish for your presence. I still ache to feel your touch, and every now and then, I swear I can hear your voice drifting on the breeze.

The memory of you remains so fresh, but memories just don't seem to be enough. The day the cancer finally claimed your body was the day that I thought I'd died as well. But I was wrong. The days and years to follow without you in my world brought a little sliver of death with each passing sunset. How would I make it in this life without you?

Then one day, someone told me, "You are so much like your mother," and suddenly it dawned on me. I would make it through life the same way you did—with unmovable faith, quiet strength, unexplainable joy, and a generous spirit.

I was married two years ago, Mama. Were you there? I placed a rose for you on the altar in the hope that God would open a window in heaven for you. I wanted you to know that I've not forgotten you. And just like you, I'm a mother. Your grandson, Michael, is almost two. I remember feeling your presence in the hospital room the day he was born. I like to think God opened another window.

Watching Michael grow and learning how to be the mother he needs is one of the most wonderful and most challenging experiences of my life. I often ask myself how in the world I can be a good mother to this precious boy, but then I remember that I have the greatest example to show me the way—you.

You were in my life such a short time, but you taught me everything I could possibly need to know. To love God, to love myself, to respect others no matter what their differences, to never give up, to believe in the unbelievable, to give generously, and to always have faith.

I'm honored when my husband tells me that I'm a great mom, because that must mean I'm a lot like you. Mama, I never did tell you all this while you were alive, but I'm hoping that God will open just one more window and allow you to read this letter so that you'll know how very, very proud of you I am. Because of the wonderful mother that you were, I am the person I am today. Thank you, Mama. Thank you for always being there when I needed you. Thank you for never giving up on me, and for loving me in a way that only you could. And most of all, thank you for allowing me to see what a truly strong and beautiful woman you were. I love you, and I'm honored that God had chosen you to show me the undying love of a mother's heart.

UNTIL WE MEET AGAIN,

Karen
Wallis, Texas

Karen Noblitt is happily married and works as a freelance writer and stay-at-home mom to three children.

It Could Have Been You

BY WENDY LYNN DECKER

Dear Mom,

"It could just as easily have been me." I wish those words ran through the minds of more people before they pass judgment on others.

When I was a young girl, you reminded me of this truth after I made a cruel and insensitive statement about another child. The young, wheelchair-bound girl with the contorted face and mangled body appeared lost inside her mind. I stared at her intently and said, "Look how creepy that girl is, Mommy. She's so ugly!"

Disheartened by my comment, you stared into my eyes and asked, "Can you see her heart?"

I chuckled. "Of course not, that's silly."

You steered me away from the child and said, "Then you shouldn't assume she's ugly, it could just as easily have been you sitting in that wheelchair. That little girl didn't choose to be born like that."

Your words struck a chord that I've sung to my entire life. As I raise my own children and battle with the day-to-day struggles of life, I often remember the moment you sparked insight into my thoughts about others. You didn't make that statement lightly, instead drawing from your own personal experiences. As a child, you were taunted by classmates because you were overweight. Abandoned by my father, you were left to raise three children alone. You only achieved an eighth-grade education and had no substantial job skills. While most women your age were comfortably married or living an independent lifestyle, you labored furiously to make ends meet.

Despite the obstacles and circumstances you were handed in life, you used every available resource to help overcome your handicaps. You raised three independent, caring children and defeated the odds against you. Little did you know that while your coping mechanisms and God carried you along, mental illness lay dormant in your mind. But despite that illness, you amazingly managed to hold down a job and take care of your home.

As I reflect on all your achievements and face the hard realization that mental illness can be inherited, I reflect that it truly could just as easily have been me in your position. I don't know that I could've handled everything life dealt you with the same strength.

Your words still echo in my mind and often flow from my mouth. When my daughter, Alyjah, made a similar remark toward another child, I shared the lesson you taught me. To my surprise, I later discovered that she too listened to your words of wisdom.

Recently Alyjah had a friend over for a visit, and as I strolled by her bedroom I caught wind of their discussion. "Did you see how dirty Brianne's clothes were?" her friend announced. "She wore them three times this week. It's like she never washes them."

"Maybe it's not her fault," Alyjah responded. "Maybe she doesn't have a washing machine; not everyone does. Or maybe it's because she doesn't have a mom."

"Still, that's just gross," the girl responded.

"You shouldn't make fun of her," Alyjah said. "It could just as easily have been you."

Alyjah's little friend looked surprised by her words—your words—and ceased gossiping about Brianne. I smiled as my heart warmed even more toward my own child, and her ability to stand up for what she believes to be right.

Your single line of wisdom is a priceless lesson that will always be a constant in the compassion that envelopes my heart. You are a woman of few words, but the ones you have spoken will go on for generations.

LOVE,

Wendy

Jackson, New Jersey

Wendy Lynn Decker is a freelance writer from New Jersey. She is author of the children's novel The Bedazzling Bowl, *and can be reached at www.wendylynndecker.com.*

The Lemonade Stand

BY ROBERTA BEACH JACOBSON

Dear Mom,

I have to admit, I owe my keen business sense to your teachings about financial management. I'm sure it was because you lived through the Great Depression that you learned to be so cautious about parting with money.

"Once your money is spent, it's gone forever," I remember you telling me.

Of course, now I understand how true you remain to your Depression-era background, but when I was a kid and heard that, I found it hardheaded. Even when I was a teen and young adult, I still didn't quite get the message.

I'm sure you remember the lemonade stand I had on those hot summer days in Ohio in the 1950s. As any third grader would, I anticipated vast profits and a booming business—every young entrepreneur's dream. To my chagrin, you had other ideas.

You calculated in advance how much "your" sugar, lemonade mix, and water would cost, and I had to pay you for my so-called business expenses out of my daily intake. Despite my protests, you held firm.

"You can't know how much you've earned until you know how much you've spent in the process," you told me. I listened impatiently. "Only then can you know what your profits truly are."

On our block, to my recollection, we sold lemonade for approximately three cents a glass. Between us kids we took in fifteen to eighteen cents each for a good day's work. But regardless of our sales, I always handed over a portion—a few pennies—to you to cover my operating expenses. Of course I griped, but to no avail.

"You'll understand the value of the lesson when you grow up," you said.

Once again, Mom, I have to admit you knew what you were talking about, although I had to grow up quite a bit for the lesson to sink in. I didn't really understand it throughout my twenties and thirties. It's possible that it wasn't until I hit forty before I finally understood your message loud and clear.

I'm not a risk taker with money. I think twice before signing any credit contracts, and I keep up on current interest rates. I shop around for bargains and sell off unwanted items rather than having them clutter up the basement. Like mother, like daughter!

I know that when I was born, you gave up your career and became a full-time mom at age forty. Because I was born premature and weighed less than three pounds, doctors told you to not expect me to survive. As a result, you never picked out a name for me and simply filled out my birth certificate using your name. For whatever reasons, I pulled through, and this is why you and I share the same name.

I want to tell you now, Mom, you've given me so much more than just your name.

With love,

Roberta

Karpathos, Greece

Roberta Beach Jacobson is an American writer who moved to Europe three decades ago. She writes short stories, articles about pets, greeting cards, and humor essays. Her Web site is www.travelwriters.com/Roberta.

Thank God for the Sandwiches

BY LAWRENCE D. ELLIOTT

Dearest Mother, Etter Jean,

Being confined to a hospital bed for four days gave me time to reflect on the influence you've had on my life, and how little I've told you given that we rarely share those feelings. But now, before anything happens to either of us, I want you to know how much you mean to me. Driving 100 miles to be by my side in the hospital was one of the many sacrifices you've made.

So many times in my life, people have wanted to change me. The values I've learned and my resistance to changing those values for anyone else are hard for people to accept. Fortunately, there have been many individuals who have admired the virtues you gave me. To both groups, I say the credit, and the blame, goes to you.

Over the years, I've had a front-row seat in watching you live your life. Your examples of responsibility, hard work, and values have been a model I've tried to emulate all my life. When we found ourselves without a warm bed, a roof over our heads, or even the knowledge of where our next meal would come from, you didn't give up. You rolled up your sleeves and went out to find a way. Fortunately, God guided a kind soul to us who temporarily opened her home to us.

Eventually we moved up to a place of our own, though it was barely large enough to fit a bed, dresser, and refrigerator. We had to maneuver carefully to get around in that room. We didn't even have a kitchen. But despite living on sandwiches, you constantly reminded us of what we had. "You should thank God for those sandwiches," you'd always say.

God must have seen how hard you worked, and sent you a friend, Brenda. Having her own family, she opened up her heart—and her small kitchen—to us. She was someone you could talk to in those days when you carried so many burdens. Later, I watched you move from job to job to improve our lives. Sometimes, you wouldn't arrive home until late at night, but not once did I see you give up. That would be yet another lesson I'd learn from you.

I used to think other kids had the nicest parents and I had the mean drill-sergeant mother who wouldn't let me have any fun. As time passed, many of those "lucky" kids were incarcerated, strung out on drugs, or dead. Reluctantly, I have to admit you were right and I was wrong.

I know we haven't seen eye-to-eye on everything, but there's one thing you'll never hear me say—that you were a bad mother. I wouldn't have become the man I've become if it weren't for you plowing away doing the dirty work. The nice house, the beautiful wife, and the career I enjoy wouldn't have been possible if it weren't for the lessons I learned from you throughout my life. Whether I was in below-zero weather on duty for the military, working long hours on my business, or in a hospital bed enduring pain, I knew I could tough it out. I had too much of you in me not to.

Recently, you were discussing your retirement, investment options, and future plans. I can't tell you how proud I was to see the woman who toiled so hard to put food on the table for her children discussing stocks and 401Ks like a pro.

This year I'll be turning forty-five, and I can't say I'm too thrilled about the prospect, but I know what you'll say: "You should be thankful God gave you those years. Some people weren't so lucky."

One thing you told me so many times has stuck with me to this day. It was a response that often came after I complained about how mean you were and how so-and-so's parents weren't so strict. You said: "You may not agree with my methods, but you won't be able to argue with the results." Once again, Mother, I have to admit you were right.

LOVE ALWAYS,
YOUR SON,

Larry
Ontario, California

Lawrence Elliott is a writer and an active realtor located in Southern California. He also runs a network of real estate Web sites accessible through www.LawrenceElliott.com.

The Best Teacher

BY BRETT J. PALANA-SHANAHAN

Dear Mom,

When I think back on my childhood and all those turbulent years growing up, one of the most vivid and precious memories I have is of you and me reading together. I remember when I was just learning to read, and every night for homework I had to read with help from an adult. At the end of each week, as proof that I'd done the assignment for the tyrannical schoolteacher, I had to turn in a slip, signed by you, listing how many hours I'd read.

I remember how you and I would sit in my bed and read so many amazing stories, like *The Lion, the Witch and the Wardrobe*, *The Borrowers*, and *Anne of Green Gables*. I looked forward to every night when I would snuggle under the covers and we could find out what happened next in those enchanting tales. You gave me a magical key that opened up new worlds and new adventures. Because of you, my imagination grew by leaps and bounds, and I fell in love with reading.

All along, as I was exploring these exciting, new worlds, you sat beside me listening as I read out loud, coaching me through tough words and correcting me when I went astray. But it was always my duty to read. You never took over, though listening to a six-year-old struggle with simple words might have been tedious or frustrating for you.

At school when we handed in our first slips, I overheard two boys talking about the reading assignments: "You read all those hours this week?" one said as he glanced over at the other's slip.

"No way, I only read a couple, and then my dad said he would just sign the slip."

But that was never the case for me. You made sure that you and I read every minute we were supposed to. Despite the fact that you worked a full day and then worked a full night at home, you always took time for our reading, and you never seemed to mind. I could tell, even at an early age, that you felt education for your children was far more important than how tired you were or anything you needed to get done around the house.

When I related to you the conversation I'd heard between the boys, you simply said, "Well, that's too bad. Those boys are only cheating themselves."

I know, Mom, why you diligently worked with me all those nights. I remember the story—the sadness of it is burned in my brain—of when you were young and wanted desperately to study botany and forestry. Your guidance counselor said: "Listen, you're a girl, you can only be a nurse or a teacher. Which one do you want to be?" Well, you didn't want to be either, but you choose to be a nurse. You excelled at nursing and grew to love it as your vocation, but you never forgot how you'd been limited in your education, and how you felt cheated out of what you dreamed of becoming. I knew you would never let that happen to your girls.

Mom, I know you read with me every night so that I would know the work it takes to be educated. I know you never let me cheat because learning was too important a gift. And I know you read with me so that when I told someone what I wanted to be when I grew up, they wouldn't have the nerve to tell me I couldn't do it.

Those nights when we read stories forever changed how I look at reading and learning, and it's why in my adult life I've come to value so deeply the time you spent with me. I know our reading influenced the many paths I would follow. My career in publishing is a direct reflection on those happy memories.

Now, as I prepare to become a mother myself, I look forward with anticipation to the time when I can read with my daughter and share the joy of learning that you instilled in me. Mom, you are more than a mother, you are a strong woman, an inspiration, a motivating force, and one of the best teachers I've ever had.

I love you Mom. Thanks for the memories!

LOVE,

Brett

Cumberland, Rhode Island

Brett J. Palana-Shanahan lives in Massachusetts with her husband, Scott, and daughter, Danica. She credits both her parents for instilling in her the importance of education and honesty.

A Proper Purse Snatching

By Karla Crawford

My Dear, Most Incredibly Proper Mother,

As I have grown older, I realize the value of the lessons that you drummed into your gangly, tomboyish daughter. For starters, you taught me the proper way to exit a vehicle without showing all of my "underthings." You also taught me the proper way to sit in a chair, sip from a glass or cup, and how to dab my mouth with a napkin. You taught me the proper fork, knife, and spoon to use at the table. And it didn't end there.

Being a proper mother, you instilled in me the proper way to put on my glove after pushing the door ringer to avoid the spot on the finger of my glove. You taught me the way to write thank-you notes, and to always remember the common courtesies that allow others to be at ease.

You also taught me the "proper" way to wreak havoc in public. Every time I see an accessories sale, Mom, I think of you and your teachings. And it was all because of a shopping excursion we embarked on many years ago.

The shop we were exploring was upscale, and the atmosphere sedate. Browsing at a table of purses, I'd pulled up the narrow strap of a soft, supple leather purse that had fallen below the surface of the heaping pile. As I looked up, you were standing on the opposite side of the table holding an exact replica of my leather strap. You looked at me with that twinkle in your eye and nonchalantly pulled your strap up higher. So I copied your actions, just as I always have. As our purse rose from the pile, other purses began to fall away. You didn't let go. And neither did I.

With a gleam in your eye and authority in your voice, you declared "It is mine." It was that gleam that I instantly recognized as the signal of a start to a mischievous war. As we bickered back and forth with ever-increasing determination the other shoppers first fell away, and then watched in what I'm sure was fascination, as two apparently well-dressed and otherwise well-behaved females argued over a single purse. I can only imagine what they were thinking as you and I continued our determined verbal battle, each of us showing no signs of willingness to relinquish our respective purse strap.

It was the appearance of a nervous store manager that provided the proverbial cherry on top. By then our audience of fellow shoppers were pretend shopping in a nice semicircle of vulturous intrigue.

You refused to let loose of your strap until I yelled out in a voice that only a pseudo adult seventeen-year-old-female can use: "Mother, I saw the purse first, and it's *mine!*"

All went silent in the store as you smiled and finally let go of your strap. The manager nearly choked, and our captive audience twittered. Until that moment we had given them no reason to believe we knew each other, much less that we were mother and daughter. Soon after, we laughed as we left the store with our purchases, off on our shopping quest for more goodies. I'm sure we left more than a few whispers behind us.

So, my dearest, proper mother, despite our purse-snatching intentions, or perhaps in spite of them, you taught me to see something of worth and reach for it. To hold on to the things I want. You taught me that a "proper" scene in public can be fun, and that being a true lady means knowing when to play like a child. To this day, that mischievous twinkle in your eye can light up my day.

I love you, Mom, for all the lessons that you taught me, and I loved that purse and carried it for years.

Karla
Oceanside, California

Karla Crawford works in commercial real estate sales and management. She enjoys reading, cooking, sewing, and, of course, shopping for accessories.

The Miracles of Mothers

BY AUDREY R.L. WYATT

Dear Mothers,

Most women are lucky to have one mother in their life. I have been blessed with three. Each of you played a special part in my life, and I am writing this letter to thank you all.

My Dear Birth Mother—you were utterly unknown to me. I pictured your face, your hair, your touch, but you were merely wisps of imagination, and I played a child's guessing game. You gave me life when you didn't have to, carried me, nourished me inside. Then you let me go, without so much as a touch or kiss good-bye. But you gave me life, and you passed me on to my adoptive mother. Thank you for that.

My Dearest Mother—you longed for me. I was a dream in your heart that couldn't come true, yet you found a way. You believed that if you wanted something truly and purely enough, it would come to you. You traveled far for me at a moment's notice.

You brought me into your life and gave me a home. We shared the same birthday, and you said I was the greatest gift you'd ever received. You cared for me, nurtured me, and helped me grow. You were there for my first step, my first day of school, my first period.

When I was sick, you sang to me, no matter that you sang off-key.

You taught me to ride a bike. You taught me to celebrate my successes, and when I had failures, you commiserated with me, encouraging me to try again. When my heart was broken, you held me and cried with me, but you never promised me it wouldn't break again.

We were a real family, as real as any other. You told me where I came from while still making me feel loved. And when Daddy died, you made sure I still felt safe and adored. When I needed him, as a willful adolescent, you did all you could to take his place. I gave you more kinds of grief than I could count, but you loved me anyway. Thank you for that.

When I became engaged, you rejoiced for me. You welcomed my fiancé into our family without hesitation, and began planning a beautiful wedding. My heart broke in a million irreparable pieces when you died before you could walk down the aisle with me. I realized then that you're never too old to need your mother.

My Dear, Dear Mother-In-Law—you embraced me when I married your only son. You took me in as your own daughter, even though you had two others. You have always been there for me, and when I became a mother, you shared your wisdom as my own mother would have. You gave me a family when mine was gone, and made me feel a part of something bigger than myself. Thank you for that.

Now that I'm a mother, I endeavor to live up to the examples set by all of you, my selfless, loving mothers. I hope that the young women I am raising will become mothers like the ones that came before them.

Thank you all for what you gave to me.

Aud

Louisville, Colorado

Audrey R.L. Wyatt has always considered herself extremely right-brained. Her passion is the written word, though she has also spent decades in children's theatre. She bases her work on her family, experiences, and culture.

My Mother, My Comfort

BY JENNIFER BROWN

Dear Mom,

It was the prettiest comforter I'd ever seen. Now, you know me. You know I'm not easily impressed by flowery, girly things. Never have been. I don't go limp-kneed at the sight of a rosebush or get gushy over lace. Normally, I would look at a comforter and say, "Yep, it's a blanket. A piece of cloth to throw over the bed." But this one was different. It was classy. It was thick and soft, with dusty colors—sage, periwinkle, mauve, and cornbread—and a pressed lacy edge that felt crisp to the touch. It was so pretty that it served as a display comforter on one of those little fake beds that line the aisles in a department store.

By all rights it was not a comforter fit for a preteen girl. I should've been sleeping under the harsh black edges of a cartoon character comforter like Strawberry Shortcake or the Care Bears like most of my friends were; dreaming of spending their days chasing after toys or boys or whatever "normal" preteen girls dreamed of.

It was almost as if you were commanding me to dream higher dreams than those girls. As if you purposely searched for and found the thickest cotton batting to use as a salve to ease the fact that my days couldn't really be spent thinking about dolls and stuffed bears. Not at that time, not with the divorce. It was as if you wanted to tell me, "Here, wrap yourself in finery and know that someday life will be fine for you again, too."

You couldn't afford that comforter. I could pretend that I've just come to that realization as an adult, but that would be a lie. I knew it then. I knew when you wrote the check at the department store register that the joy in your eyes from buying me such a special gift was tinged with worry.

I could have told you not to buy it, to go to the nearest discount store and buy a Strawberry Shortcake comforter. But I knew that you needed to give me this wonderful comforter just as much as I needed it. I needed to wrap myself in those dreams, and you needed to assure yourself that you could still provide me with them. I let you buy it because it was our affirmation to one another that both our lives were going to get better: mine through the sheer passage of time, and yours by the fact that you could still give me things that mattered most to you—pride, hope, and vision.

I watched you as you pressed the wrinkles out of the dust ruffle and spread the new comforter across my bed, showing me that despite your personal devastation, you could still make life pretty. I learned to watch you in other ways, too. Family members say that I'm the independent one—the one who nobody has to worry about. The one who gets things done, who will always be okay. I could silently pretend that I was born with that trait. But the truth is, I learned it from you, Mom.

My ability to forge ahead, even through the barest of times, to laugh in the face of hardship, to keep myself in a position of control over my destiny—all of those qualities about me that I consider most "me," I learned from you. From watching the worry battle your joy while writing a check, to watching you smooth out the comforter on the bed as if spreading out my future in sage, periwinkle, mauve, and cornbread, to wrapping myself up in that small luxury of cotton and lace. I wasn't born independent. I just paid attention. I listened, even when you weren't speaking—especially when you weren't speaking.

I still keep that comforter in a special place. I never use it on a bed. I hope I never have to. But, rest assured, Mom, it's there, and always will be, just in case. A legacy from mother to child. A lesson in encouragement and belief. A study in perseverance.

After all, it's not just a blanket—not just a piece of cloth to throw over the bed.

LOVE,

Jennifer
Liberty, Missouri

Two-time winner of the Erma Bombeck global humor contest, Jennifer Brown lives, writes, and makes her mother proud in Liberty, Missouri.

3.

You Are My Hero

A hero by his or her very nature is often a larger-than-life character, one whose tale revolves around a journey that takes him or her from one place and time to another. Almost always, a hero accomplishes amazing feats, endures tumultuous times, and is ultimately a better person as a result of the experience.

Mothers are heroes. They give us birth, nurture our minds and bodies, heighten our spirit in times good and bad, and permeate our souls with unconditional love. In having us they surrender part of themselves, but give it freely and without hesitation. They are teachers, who by their actions introduce us to the world and all its kind and sometimes harsh realities. They show us how to be strong, how to live, how to treat others, and how to survive.

As heroes traverse their paths, they are in a constant search for knowledge, their vision guiding them to places and situations they've never before encountered. Our mothers are graced with the wisdom of the ages, of all the mothers who came before them. They give us the gift of insight, and the ability to dream higher than they ever dared. In doing so, they will forever remain our heroes.

My Mother's Gloves

BY MARIA MCCOOL

Dear Mom,

It was three years ago in January that you left us, and I couldn't imagine what life would be like without you. You were a stay-at-home mom to an only child, and to say that I was the center of attention, deeply cherished, and unconditionally loved is a huge understatement.

At times I felt it was a burden being an only child. I felt it was up to me to preserve the balance of emotional well-being in our family. I grew up playing the role of negotiator. But I believe that helped me to develop empathy and a maturity beyond my years, and I seem to have the ability to say just the right thing to someone, to help them feel better about themselves, their pain, or a difficult situation they find themselves in.

Although you suffered many disappointments in life from childhood through adulthood, you never lost your ability to give love, nourishment, and care to family and friends. You could always burst out in laughter, flash your billion-watt smile, or light up the dance floor—with or without a partner.

I remember you as a lady who could wear a wide-brimmed hat and sport white gloves, yet run to the aid of a child who had been hurt in an automobile accident. I remember that day clearly. You, Dad, and I were

walking down the main business street in our
neighborhood en route to visit Daddy's sister, Aunt
Annie, who had an apartment above one of the retail
stores. It was a beautiful, sunny, and quiet Sunday
afternoon, and we were happily walking down the street.
I was skipping, holding on to your white-gloved hand
on one side and grasping Daddy's hand on the other.

Piercing this peaceful, happy scene was a terrible
screeching sound. You and Daddy quickly turned
around. Daddy ran out into the street as you pulled me
into the doorway of Aunt Annie's apartment. You
hurriedly rang the bell, and when she answered, you
told me to go inside. Then you ran back to where
Daddy was kneeling in the street.

I played with Lady, Aunt Annie's dog, not really
sure what was happening. But I will always remember
what you looked like when you finally walked through
the doorway. Your stylish hat remained straight atop
your head, but you'd removed your white gloves. You
told me that a little boy on a bicycle had been hit by a
car, and Daddy was waiting with him and the small
crowd that had gathered until the ambulance came to
take him to the hospital.

You didn't say much more, but I glanced at your
purse. There peeking out of the top were your white
gloves, only now they weren't white at all—they were
red, with bloody spots all over them. I was riveted by
the sight of them. I couldn't turn away. Until I saw those

gloves, the little boy in the street wasn't real, but those gloves painted a picture of how badly hurt he was. I couldn't stop thinking and worrying about him. It took a long time for me to fall asleep that night, but you lay with me and together we prayed for the little boy.

Long after you washed the stains of that day from your gloves, I remembered how quickly you ran to help someone else's child. I understood how your proper manners and fine clothing didn't stop you from trying to help a hurt and frightened child whose own mother was not there to comfort him.

Every time I think back on that day, I see those gloves. I feel the warmth of your cheek on mine as you cradled me in your arms, and I feel the tenderness and strength in your ungloved hands. I knew those hands would keep me safe from danger and my fears. I also remember the lesson I learned firsthand that day, of how to truly live by the Golden Rule.

YOUR LOVING DAUGHTER,

Maria
Pittsburgh, Pennsylvania

Maria McCool lives in Pittsburgh with her husband, children, and dog, Sydney. She is the author of Becoming George's Brother, *a work she created to preserve her father's memories and her family history.*

The Swiss Miss

BY BARB KARG

Dear Ma,

There isn't a day that goes by that I don't thank you for being Swiss. You may think I love being Swiss because of the chocolate, and while that can't be entirely denied, it is most certainly not the reason for my pride. In fact, chocolate is a mere culinary influence that barely scratches the surface of how I pay tribute to your legacy, and the values, ethics, and moral code you passed on to me. Like a Swiss watch, I keep time by your standards.

You immigrated to the States in 1959, leaving family, friends, your entire world. At age twenty-three, that took amazing strength, courage, and ambition. To this day, I remain in awe of your bravery and ability to not only think outside the box, but send it packing, loaded down with closed-minded perceptions.

While I was still vacationing in your womb, you were already speaking to me in Swiss German. By our second trip to visit your mother, *Omi,* in Switzerland, I was not only fluent, but I had your dialect. That is something I treasure.

Throughout my childhood, you and Pop filled our home with culture, worldly insight, and language. Whenever friends and family visited us, the air was blessed with the melodic, animated purr of German,

Italian, and French. It was pure magic. By exposing me
to so much culture, you provided me a wider view of a
world that I may not otherwise have had the chance to
explore, much less understand.

In a broad sense, you allowed me to understand that
there are many opinions, views, and ways to do things.
And in a narrow sense, you reminded me on a daily
basis that I'm a citizen of a culture whose common
courtesy and practicality are matched only by its
tenacity to keep life, love, friends, family, and the entire
world in clear perspective. From you I learned about
and highly prize being awarded the liberty of an
American and a well-grounded Swiss. And it's all the
better that Pop's German ways added to the mix.

Having grown up in the States, but in an
environment permeated with European tradition and
sensibility, my upbringing might be considered
unconventional at times by some folks. Christmas, for
example was very different in the Karg household. With
just the four of us in this country, we didn't have the
flood of relatives most American families had. We
celebrated St. Nikolaus Day, where every December
sixth, you had Little Sis and I lay out our empty shoes
by the fireplace. By morning, they would be brimming
with chocolate, nuts, and fruit. European tradition was
important to you.

When Sis and I relentlessly implored you to buy a
Christmas tree after Thanksgiving, you held firm. We
didn't get that tree until Christmas Eve, and we

decorated it together as a family. And prior to opening gifts, we had to sing at least three Christmas carols in German. Our evening was then followed by a sumptuous feast of boiled potatoes, liverwurst, and limburger, after which we played games together. To this day I've never heard a human being laugh as hard as you did when we played Pig Mania. Who knew a handful of little pink plastic oinkers playing *cirque du-pork* on our dining-room table could trigger such laughter from a normally reserved Swiss lady?

Ma, to me you are a mother beyond measure. A woman with the grace and charm of Audrey Hepburn, the quiet wisdom of Ghandi, and the practicality and panache of Erma Bombeck. You have the business sense of a CFO, the creativity of a French artiste, and a quiet but deadly sense of humor.

It's easy to think small and see life through a telescope, always seeing what happens outside your realm, but never truly understanding how other people and the rest of the world lives. You gave me one of the greatest gifts a person could receive—the foresight and gumption to look beyond the seas, beyond moral and ethical borders, and beyond any measure of black and white. Because of you, I see the world and everything and everyone in it through unbiased eyes. My individual nature comes from you.

I am, and shall always be, in awe of your intelligence, courage, grace, and pure kindness of your soul. I am your Swiss Miss, and despite all humorous attempts to deny it, I am most definitely and very happily and proudly your eldest daughter. Thank you for all you've done for me, Ma. For so unconditionally gifting me and showing me who you are and who I am. Through thick and thin you've been my rock. I can't imagine that you're as proud of me as I am of you.

Alle meine liebe,

Barb
Depoe Bay, Oregon

Barb Karg is a veteran journalist, author, graphic designer, and screenwriter. She resides in the Pacific Northwest with her better half, Rick, and five four-legged children. Because of her mother, she remains a chocolate snob to this day.

Sink or Swim

BY REBEKAH BURGWEGER

Dear Mom,

I just wanted to thank you for all these things you done
for me. I remember when I was swimming at the
McClintic's lake. You thought that my friend Kenzie was
pulling me under the water, so you jumped in the lake as
fast as you could without thinking of taking off your
clothes and putting on your bathing suit. You didn't even
take off your shoes! You pulled me to the dock as fast as
you could. But when you got us out, Dad and everyone
else said that Kenzie was not pulling me down.

You were probably embarrassed and thought that I
would never understand why you did that. Well I do! You
love me and don't want me to die. You were afraid I was
getting pulled down under and you jumped in to save me.
Now I know how much you love me! Thank you Mom!

LOVE,

Rebekah

De Soto, Kansas

Rebekah Burgweger is almost ten years
old. She loves her four bunnies, and loves
to write and read lots of books. She loves
animals, but loves bunnies the most!

Best of the Best

BY BRENDAN O'NEILL

Dear Mom,

I just wanted to let you know I thought of you the other day. Not because I was looking at a picture, or reading a card you sent, or thinking about a trip home. No. It definitely was none of those. I thought of you the other day when I was trying to cook dinner, in between switching my laundry from the washer to the dryer, while figuring out how to manage paying my rent, loans, and credit card bill. And all I could think of was:

How did she do this for four other people?

Sure, growing up, Pat, Terry, and I pitched in . . . occasionally. And Dad tried—he really did—but he would get so preoccupied with one task, he'd forget about the other 746 still to do. No, it was definitely you Mom, juggling your four guys and their four lives, complete with ironing and math homework, ski practice, and lasagna dinners. Oh, and your teaching school five days a week.

The other day after work, all I wanted to do was go home and relax. But I realized that unless I wanted to smell like a hamper the next day, I had a load of laundry to do. Damn it. Then I stopped myself. One load of laundry?

I was complaining about one load of laundry?

You would come home from an exhausting day of teaching high school, do two loads before starting dinner, and not even blink. Living away from home, I finally realized something, and it wasn't that I was without a live-in maid—someone to clean, cook, and do everything else in between. No, Mom, I realized you were an extremely strong and driven individual who was utterly and unflinchingly dedicated to making sure everything was perfect for her family.

It's not like we took you for granted—we at least tried to help out. But the pleats were never as crisp, the casserole's edges always ended up a bit burnt, and scraps of food still stuck to the dishes even after we put them through the washer. You did everything the best. And wanted the best. And always made sure everything was the best.

I just want to let you know that you're the best. Not because you did everything and anything for us with a perfect smile and wonderful poise. You weren't some sort of Stepford Mom, chained to her ironing board awaiting the next command. No, you're the best because you always wanted the best for your boys.

From discipline to education, all three of us were made to walk a very fine line. You made sure our homework wasn't just done, but that it was done well; we never misbehaved (at least not in public); and we were sure to do the best we could do in whatever we were doing.

Your strive for perfection has fueled mine. And knowing that you've done everything I have to do, but four-fold, makes me want to strive harder—without complaint. You're amazing Mom, and I just wanted to let you know.

LOVE,

Brendan

Boston, Massachusetts

Brendan O'Neill was born and raised in Western Massachusetts. He now lives in Boston and works in the publishing industry.

As Good As It Gets

BY KRISTA CLAIRE HOLT

Dear Mom,

Your granddaughter Maisy was only eight months old
when you were first diagnosed with ovarian cancer. As I
look back now, I see that the lives of my two young
children have been formed by my taking care of you as
you faced this terminal illness. Your four-year battle
with ovarian cancer has ended, but I see that your many
gifts are being carried on.

In your final years, it was clear that your family was a
precious lifeline, helping anchor you to this place, this
life. Sick or well, you savored time with your family and
made it your first priority.

Whether we were simply sharing an overnight stay
at one of our homes or vacationing on the coast, you
would frequently say, "This is as good as it gets. It doesn't
get any better than this."

Your second surgery to remove tumors in your
abdomen, intestines, and colon was scheduled shortly
before the delivery date of my second born, Miles. I
recall your discussion with the surgeon, asking how
realistic it was to be present at your grandchild's birth
just six weeks after major surgery. You set your sights
on that goal and marched toward it, ready for a quick
recovery and full participation in life.

The day I went into labor, you were ready. You jumped in your car, made the two-hour drive, and sat by my side as I labored into the night. You were determined to be there for me and to welcome your grandson into the world. I believe that family had become central to your survival. And now, as I'm reeling from the grief of losing you, I can see that my family is central to my own.

Over the last four years, I watched you gracefully survive three surgeries and cope with nearly 100 days of chemotherapy, months of radiation, and the slow decline of your health. At the weekly cancer support group I attended, I shared my concerns about being absent from my babies so much of the time while caring for my ill mother, and how, even when my children were with me, I still needed to focus on you.

A wise, older woman in the group quietly shook her head, patted my hand, and said, "You, my dear, are teaching your babies what it is to love one's mother. You are showing them how to take care of you when the time comes."

I will never forget the day that my little four-year-old Maisy accompanied you to chemo. As you were holding my hand and grimacing from the pain of the infusion needle, Maisy reached over to hold your other hand and said, "You are so brave, Nonnie. I love you. I hope you feel better."

I see now that they were learning priceless lessons about caring for family, and that they recognized the value of being there for someone you love.

Maisy and Miles knew that when they visited you at your home they would find you in the bed we'd arranged in the living room. They loved to snuggle up with you and read stories. The attention you gave them was remarkable, despite a head full of Vicodin and a body full of aches and pains. No one listens to us quite like our mothers, or grandmothers. You gave your grandchildren the gifts of listening and paying close attention to who they were. They loved you madly for that, as did I.

And so I thank you, Mom, for being with me for the birth of my babies and for allowing me to blossom as a mother at my own speed and in my own way. I thank you, Mom, for allowing me to share, so vulnerably, in your final journey—a courageous journey that revealed your perseverance, endurance, and character. You served as a model for both living fully and dying peacefully.

On our final trip together as a family, you overheard me singing Miles a lullaby and you asked me to sing it to you. I sang it to you that night, trying to get it out through the tears that were welling in my eyes. During your last two days with us, I sang the same lullaby to you over and over, and I believe in my heart that it brought you comfort as you drifted in and out of consciousness.

Maisy and Miles ask for that lullaby every night as I tuck them into bed. Two-year-old Miles has even started singing it with me in the last few weeks. It's as though you are there, humming along as Miles sings with me.

You told us before you died that your spirit would hover over us. Now Maisy and Miles speak about you living in their hearts.

I see your generous, caring ways in them, and I can't help but smile and think, "This is as good as it gets. It doesn't get any better than this."

YOURS ALWAYS,

Krista Claire
Santa Cruz, California

Krista Claire Holt grew up in the San Francisco Bay Area. She taught kindergarten and first grade for thirteen years and is now home with her two young children, humbled by the work and the beauty of it all.

Wind Beneath My Wings

BY LOIS JOAN NOORMAN WENCIL

Hi Mommy,

There are so many things I wish I'd told you when we were together, but as a mother and daughter team it's never too late. You nurtured me with the sunshine of your smile, your known and unknown tears, your never-ending love, and the strength of your faith in my success.

You graduated from elementary school and then went to work in the Patterson silk mills in New Jersey. You and Dad married, and I was a love child with a stay-at-home Mom. You took care of me and my grandparents. I can still hear you say, "Taking care of our responsibilities is why we were put here. That includes our family, and everything and everybody in our home." Our cousins, siblings, and neighbors knew that help and a good meal could always be found in your kitchen.

After cancer took my sight, you and Dad decided that I'd be your only child. I had a dozen cousins to keep me company, and that was fine with me. "One perfect daughter is all any couple deserves, so we can't be greedy. We've got the best," you'd always say. And you stuck to that philosophy.

You refused to send me away to a school for the blind. Instead, you found a class that taught Braille in a local public school. Unconditional love didn't get in the way of my education. You never made me do chores, but we both know that my homework was a different story. You always said, "If you haven't an understanding of where you've come from, and the educational tools to handle what is and may come, you'll never get where you have to go."

You never missed a beat. You taught me the oral history of our ancestors, including the stowaways who fled from the potato famine in Ireland. Then the marooned English seaman on Henry Hudson's 1609 *Half Moon* voyage who married a maiden of the Munsi Clan in the Lenape tribe of the Delaware Nation. You told me about Laura, the idolized star who sang soprano at the Fabian Opera House in eighteenth-century Patterson, and Grandma Alice—our own runaway bride—who gave up a life of privilege to marry a jobless ex-sailor.

You also told me how you met Dad at a church supper and fell in love at first sight, and how one July evening the stork found the most perfect pink baby on the baby tree and brought me to you to make our family complete. You emphasized that I must remember these stories and tell them to my own little girl. You assured me of my place in our ancestral line, and I've begun to pass these legends on to my own perfect daughter. Fact or fiction, they are the basis for my historical romance series.

You always took pride in my learning and taught me homemaking skills. You never owned your own home, but you bought my accordion and had it imported from Italy. You never had the chance to further your education, but on each of my graduation days I gave you my degrees. You made sure I got to school, music lessons, and church on time, and you taught me that "amusements are more fun when all your work is done."

I wandered away, as all adolescents do, but you taught me that "it's okay to disagree with those in authority if you can understand why your beliefs differ from theirs. Rebellion for its own sake is a wasted effort." No matter what my crusade or excuse for doing what I wanted, you were always there for me.

In time, I began to travel with a guide dog, progressed in a career in education, married, and had children. Still you and I shared day-to-day happenings. You heard my frustrations. We shared my fears. You did what best friends and mothers do—you listened. Your advice was the sugar in my tea, never the salt in my wound. "It's okay to fall down as long as you get up to try again," you often told me.

In time, you developed Alzheimer's, which robbed you of your ability to maintain your home and yourself. It stole your memories. So I told and retold the old stories to you, and for as long as you knew me to be your daughter, you gave me whatever was left of your spirit. We replaced shopping malls with nursing home halls, but we walked together until you slipped away.

Roots and wings are the gifts of a true parent. You grounded me in lifelong learning, a work ethic, and the importance of family. My wings were my education, my freedom to grow and then go, and the knowledge that even now you are somewhere still watching over me and applauding whatever I do, right or wrong.

Thank you. I miss you every day.

YOUR DAUGHTER,

Lois
Millburn, New Jersey

Lois Joan Noorman Wencil is a daughter, wife, mother, sister, friend, teacher, and published author—none of which would have been as fulfilling without her Mom.

The Mastery of Grace

BY SULOCHANA VINAYAGAMOORTHY

Dear *Amma*,

You lived your life simply and humbly, and with love and honor you were buried. At the peak of ethnic war, and amid shell blasts and an around-the-clock curfew in Jaffna, Sri Lanka, you passed away after a brief illness without having a chance to say good-bye to me. Because of the war, phone lines were cut off, flights were canceled, and buses and trains stood immobile. I lived 500 kilometers from you, and in no way could I know about your death until a month later.

You probably heard the sound of my wail blasting through the sky and reaching you in heaven when news of your death hit my ears. Oh, how I wish I could've told you how much I savored your unconditional love and outstanding patience. Regrettably, in my ignorance, I took it for granted that you understood my gratitude, and failed to express it in words while you were still alive.

Today, being a mom, I know how enticing the words "I love you, Mom," and "Thank you, Mom" are to a mother's ears. If I'd have known better, I would've showered you with such words, and even written countless poems to gladden your heart, instead of the gifts and cards I dutifully sent you only on special days.

You weren't a regular churchgoer, as your arthritic feet throbbed with pain whenever you tried to walk the distance to the nearby church. Yet, your love for God didn't dwindle for lack of fellowship at church. I remember well your two favorite sayings: "He who took care of us in the past would take care of us in the future too," and "Without God's permission, nothing could happen to us." You didn't utter them just to feel good or to bring momentary comfort to those around you. Instead you modeled to us how truly you believed in what you said.

Of the forty years I had known you, never did I see anger paint your face, nor anxiety cloud your eyes. Even when the sudden death of John, your beloved son and my brother, hit you like a tornado, you remained stoic. Instead of crawling into a corner and questioning God's fairness, you faced the loss with grace and gave us the strength to bear the pain. You probably assumed that it happened with the Almighty's permission, and consoled your grieving heart with words from the Holy Bible.

Do you know that when my husband came to Christ, he counted you as one of the key players in leading him down this path? I found it hard to believe at first, for I never saw you talk to him about Christ or quote Bible verses to convince him. Yet your graceful actions must have spoken to him more effectively than any words. Truly, you must have modeled what Saint

Francis of Assisi taught: "Preach always. Use words only when needed."

Apart from your faith and amazing patience, you possessed another quality, which I admired the most. During all the years I lived with you, I never heard you speak ill of any person. Gossiping never had a chance to enter your presence. I clearly recall a day when I was twelve, when a few of our neighbors came to visit you for mid-morning tea and chat. During the conversation, one woman started talking about a teenage girl who had eloped with her math tutor the previous night. Any other woman would have cupped her hands around her ears to hear better or added to the talk—but not you, *Amma*. From the adjacent room, I heard you boldly put a stop to the chatter by saying, "We aren't sure what our children are going to do in the future, so let us not talk about others' children, especially anything bad about them." You had no knowledge how deeply those words, still etched in my mind, have guarded me from indulging in any kind of gossip.

Amma, by being passive and soft spoken you remained invisible even in a known circle. You hadn't done anything extraordinary to gain people's applause. In today's world, you wouldn't have had a chance to compete for "Super Mom" in a contest. Yet, in my view, you're worthy of being inducted into the Hall of Fame for Mothers, for being the mother that God wanted you to be. I pen this letter to you with a heart full of thanks, and to tell you how much I miss you in every stage of my life.

I LOVE YOU,

Kunju
Saskatoon, Canada

Freelance writer, poet, and columnist Sulochana Vinayagamoorthy is a member of Inscribe Christian Writer's Fellowship. Her work has appeared in several Christian magazines. She enjoys reading, baking, being outdoors, and spending time with her family.

From the Heart

BY ETHAN WHITE

Mom,

I mis you and I Lov you to! I lov to cudl yith you! I prod of you fer chiring fer me when I hit the ball. I lov you yith all of my hart!

XOXO

Ethan White is a six-year-old with a big heart. He's always writing his mommy love letters. He enjoys playing baseball, swimming, and karate. He wants to help people when he grows up, but he hasn't figured out what Jesus wants him to do yet.

The Road Less Traveled

BY CAROLYN PAYNE-SORRELL

Dear Momma,

As a young woman, I loved to hear you tell the story of
how you drove our old tractor, pulling a high trailer
filled with just-plucked cotton. It was the late 1940s, I
was just a kid, and Daddy had a nervous breakdown.
We were poor farmers in East Texas, and the cotton crop
had just been harvested. There was no one to take it to
town so it could be sold, and those few dollars the
cotton would bring were all that stood between
starvation and us. You took it upon yourself to do it.

It was a chilly fall day, and you could see your breath
in front of your face. You dressed in the warmest overalls
and flannel shirt you could find—Daddy's clothes—and
took off down the dirt road in front of our old farmhouse.

When you reached the highway you made better
time, but even then it took the better part of half a day
to get to the city of Kaufman, where the cotton gin
was. Your arrival caused quite a stir because no one had
ever seen a woman driving a tractor to town before. In
those days, women were still stuck in the kitchen,
baking and herding "young-uns."

You were chilled all the way through by the time
you reached the gin mill, and kept getting colder as you
waited for the trailer to be weighed and unloaded.

When you finally got the money for the cotton, you glanced across the street and saw a small neon sign in the window of the only café in town. It proclaimed good news: *Hot Steaming Cup of Coffee—Only a Nickel.*

For several moments all the pros and cons raced through your head. You studied your hands, half-frozen and numb even through your thick brown gloves. *Only a nickel,* you thought over and over. But then you remembered your husband, ill at home in bed, and your three babies who'd been living on scrambled eggs for more than a week, thanks to a single good old laying hen.

You turned away from the café and the thoughts of hot coffee and climbed back onto the tractor, carefully folding your cash and tucking it safely away. You drove all the way home and arrived just before dark, cold through and through, with nothing waiting for supper except eggs. Even so, you had to clean up and get to the kitchen to prepare them yourself before anyone would get anything to eat.

Momma, this story always inspired me to reach further and try harder. You were always that spunky redhead who was willing and ready to do whatever had to be done. You loved adventure and searched for it in each simple act.

Thank you, Momma, for teaching me to take the road less traveled. Thanks for teaching me to enjoy life's moments. Somehow you managed to find joy in every detail of life. No matter how grueling the chore, you knew how to turn it into a fun-filled escapade.

The lessons you taught me have served me well throughout my life. I'm sorry I never told you just how much I appreciated you, and the example you set for us kids.

I love you and still miss you even now,

Carolyn
Dallas, Texas

Poet, novelist, and short story writer Carolyn Payne-Sorrell was raised in East Texas. She enjoys painting and woodworking. To supplement her income, she works as a disaster housing inspector for FEMA.

Call of the Wild

By Gregory Bergman

Dear Mom,

Who versus whom.

That versus which.

And the rule of three.

Do I use the last comma in a series or not? As Managing Editor of *EQUITIES* magazine, I don't. As an author, I do. When in doubt, I call my mom.

Ring. Ring. Ring.

"Hello, darling," you always say. You know I'm calling for help.

"Hi, Mom."

"How are you, darling?"

"Good. Quick question. I'm about to send this article to print and I'm not sure about this sentence. Is it who or whom: 'The new CEO whom management believes will pull them out of the red' or 'The new CEO who . . .'"

"What about 'Management believes this new CEO will pull the company out of the red?'"

"Oh, yeah. And you're sure that's . . ."

"I'm sure."

"Okay, thanks, Mom."

Five minutes later.

"This is Paula."

"Hi, Mom."

"Yes, darling. I'm busy, what is it?"

"Quick question. What's correct: 'The new product which was released last spring is expected to generate record profits.' Or is it that?"

"That. That is restrictive, which is unrestrictive, remember?"

"Oh, yeah. Thanks, Mom. Sorry."

I hang up the phone.

Thirty minutes later.

I can't call you again, you'll kill me. You have other writers to worry about, writers you get paid to help. But I can't seem to finish this story. I wish there were someone else I could ask, but there's no one as good as you are. Damn.

Ring. Ring. Ring.

"This is Paula."

"Hi, Mommy."

Sigh. "Hello, darling."

"Mom, I'm in trouble. I can't seem to finish this story and I have half an hour to turn it in. The ending is terrible, the beginning is stupid, and the middle is a mess. It's awful."

"No, it isn't. It's fine. Now calm down."

"Mom, I can't do it. I need help!"

"Stop it. Relax. I can't help you right now, I'm too busy."

"Mom, I've tried and I can't do this in time. I'm going to get fired!"

"Stop being such a baby. You're not going to get fired and you are going to finish it and it will be fine."

"But Mom . . ."

"Stop whining. You know what to do, so do it! I have to go. I'm busy."

You hang up on me.

Finally, the rule of three is satisfied, and I can get down to work. I wrap it up in fifteen minutes and, as you've predicted, the story is fine. I've always whined and complained and relied on your scolding to motivate me. But a year ago it wasn't this easy on either of us. I wasn't whining on the phone from across the country, I was whining right from your living room couch.

You were so proud of me—your son, the college graduate. It took me long enough; after attending three community colleges in three different states, I managed to transfer to Hunter College where I finally graduated at age twenty-four. That was the good news. The bad news was that I majored in philosophy, a degree that's worth little in the real world. After a year of telemarketing jobs, I did what anyone would do—I called my mom.

The view from your couch was perfect for writing, at least that's what you told me. Peering out of those big antique windows, you could spend a whole day just watching the lake. I spent a year. It was the perfect setting for an aspiring writer and philosopher king.

Again, your words. But you were right. You got me a job writing *The Little Bathroom Book of Philosophy* for your publishing company. I was sure that I couldn't write it but you were just as sure that I could. After all, not only did I know my philosophy, the bathroom was only a few steps away from the couch.

As I whined my way through 50,000 words, the "I can'ts" and "I'm no goods" and "I'm an idiots" slowly began to fade away into the mist over the lake. Okay, so my metaphors still need work.

Ring. Ring. Ring.

Talk to you soon, Ma.

LOVE,

Greg
Los Angeles, California

Gregory Bergman is a writer and editor. The author of The Little Bathroom Book of Philosophy *and* Isms—from Autoeroticism to Zoroastrianism, *he currently serves as Managing Editor of* EQUITIES *magazine, a financial publication based in Southern California where he lives and works.*

Caravans of Life

By Sonja Herbert

Dear *Mutti*,

As long as I can remember, I wanted to write a book about the story of your life. Even as a little girl, living as part of our traveling carnival in Germany with my three sisters and two brothers, I wanted the world to know what you went through to escape Hitler. Now that I'm an adult, I appreciate your experiences even more.

It took me several years, but now the story is finished. I finally see the determination and love you had to raise six children in the direst of circumstances. All of us became healthy, loving, and successful individuals, and for that, I thank you.

I remember the circus you and *Vati* owned when I was small, but I can't remember when I first learned that in your youth, you hid inside this same circus during the Holocaust, or when I first knew I'd one day write your story. When you visited me several years ago in Utah, you finally told me of your travails. I tape recorded what you told me, and heard many things I didn't know.

You were raised in Berlin, the center of the Third Reich, by your Aryan mother. You told me how much you missed your Jewish father, my grandfather, who died when you were only four years old, before Hitler came to power. I hadn't known how harsh and unloving your own mother was, how she sent you for hours to play on the streets so she could go out with her friends. When your mother remarried, to an Aryan, and had another daughter with blonde hair and blue eyes, she became even colder to you, the dark-eyed, dark-haired daughter who wasn't approved of by society.

Later, as you grew older and things became difficult, you had to find safety for yourself. I listened, spellbound, as you told me of your decision to apply for a job with a traveling circus to get away from the Nazis. I learned about the circus manager who gave you a choice—either become his mistress, or be sent to a concentration camp. In spite of your youth, you outwitted him, kept your dignity, and remained hidden in the circus. You even found your true love during that harrowing time, the man who owned the circus and would become my father.

As I learned about your life, my own childhood came into focus. I remembered our carnival with the merry-go-round and the shooting hall, which *Vati* acquired after he lost the circus, and the overcrowded situation in our caravan home. We had no money, and hardly a home, but I can't remember a moment I felt hungry or unsafe. Without a complaint, you washed diapers in a bucket, picked dandelion greens, and plucked chickens on the caravan's doorsteps for our dinners. You worked at the shooting hall on the weekends while still keeping an eye on all six of us. And after every exhausting day you slept with father on the pull-out sofa in the living room, while we were safe and warm in the bedroom compartment of the caravan, two of us in each bed.

Later while transcribing the tape, I saw you as a girl who struggled to stay alive and get a measure of joy out of the most difficult circumstances—a young woman abandoned by her family, who never gave up. And that's how you raised us. You never gave up.

When we four girls were teenagers, you decided to quit traveling with the carnival to give us a more steady home. You found an apartment for us, and let us have the choice to travel with our father, or stay and live a life we previously had only dreamed of. I thank you for that, too. Because you gave me that choice, I found a church and gave myself to Christ. You might still not approve of that decision I made so long ago, but I know you approve of what I did with my life and how I lived it.

The story of your youth is finished. I see your character and your determination, and the way you raised us, better than your own mother raised you— and under much worse circumstances.

I too believe that I have done better as a mother. I learned my own determination from you. Finally, I see you as the person you are, and not just as my mother, and it doesn't matter if we don't always see eye to eye.

Our love and respect for each other bridges those differences.

WITH LOVE,

Sonja
Hillsboro, Oregon

Sonja Herbert has written several award-winning stories, essays, and a novel about her mother's life during the Holocaust. Her memoir about her childhood in a traveling carnival is almost finished. Her Web site is www. Germanwriter.com.

As Love Shines

BY BETH THOMPSON

Dear Mother,

As Love Shines. That is your lasting gift to me. Darkness
comes, but the promise of light is always there, shining
through the stars.

I think of this each evening as the bruised sky purples
into night, and the stars come out, free for the taking.
Your bright star—the one I chose as a symbol of our
lasting mother-daughter bond—the one I talk to, appears
shining brightly, reminding me that love endures beyond
the boundaries of life. As Love Shines, it never dies.

As Love Shines—ALS. Those three letters tried to
define the last years of your life with an illness so cruel
and intractable, it shook all our lives to the core. A
baseball hero from years ago became a familiar name
and face as we searched for information about those
dreaded letters, Amyotrophic Lateral Sclerosis,
commonly known as Lou Gehrig's Disease. To our
dismay, we learned there was no cure.

As you lost the use of your hands, your legs, and
finally your voice and ability to swallow, your mind and
spirit still shone through as brightly as any celestial
point of light. From the early days of noticing the
tremor in your beautifully handwritten letters, until the
final days when you were too weak to walk and light

enough for me to carry, your spirit shone through it all.
It gave new meaning to the letters ALS. *As Love Shines*
gave all of us courage to face the coming night.

The last year, which could have been all about dying,
was really all about learning to live so fiercely, so purely,
that death became only a way station on a never-ending
journey. As you handed off your lasting love to me, so
will I hand off mine to my girls, Jamie and Megan, who
love you so, and keep your star shining in their hearts.
Eternal life is all about eternal love, but it is treasured in
mortal moments, and in the hearts left behind.

ALS as a disease did not define you and could not
contain you. You laughed in the face of it. When your
dedicated physician, Dr. Norris, described to you an
imbalance in the electrolytes of your body chemistry,
you made him smile by joking about your "electric
lights." There was more truth to that than you knew.

Luminescent. That's how your face became, and
how I see you still.

You and I were always close, the love was always
there, but often in my tumultuous transition from child
to young adult, our words were heated, cutting, and
ended in tears. Mothers give advice unasked, and
daughters resist taking it. That's the way of it for
mother and daughter during the growing-up years,
because we both had growing up to do.

One thing you always believed in was my writing,
and you delighted in my successes, as mothers do. Years
later, I found a notebook with your own early attempts

at writing. Near the end, when that most unexpected surprise arrived—my winning a major writing award—your hands were already too weak to hold the golden statue with its lightning wings. "I always knew you'd win!" you said. And the light in your eyes said the rest. As Love Shines.

After your death, I had to face my own threatening alphabet. First, AN (acoustic neuroma), a benign brain tumor that threatened my hearing, and then BC (breast cancer), a malignant tumor that threatened my life. I really needed your star then, so I made my own letters stand for "Alive, Now!" and "Believe, Courage!"

Mother, I can't hand you this tribute about the letters of our lives, and the love that endures, but as I pass along the love to my girls, they'll see that life never really ends as long As Love Shines.

MUCH LOVE,

Beth

Sonoma, California

Beth Thompson is a freelance author, poet, an Emmy winner, and a teacher and private tutor in Sonoma, California. Her life centers around her supportive husband, Blair, and her two remarkable daughters, Jamie and Megan.

4.

You Are Always in My Heart

All creatures great and small have a bond with their mother, a tie that is unwavering in its simplicity. As we mature, we bear witness to a mother's grace under pressure and her never-ending strength. Mothers raise us to be worthy individuals and elevate us to heights of spirituality that we might never have attained without their unwavering support. They encourage us to follow our dreams, and hold our hands through our darkest nights.

Many of us strive to truly understand our mothers, a feat that at times seems unattainable. We want answers to questions that we don't yet know how to ask, but in the end does that really matter? The journey that mother and child take binds them inseparably from one lifetime to the next throughout the generations and it's the memories created along the way that allow us to truly see our mothers.

As we grow from child to adult, we realize that our mother is the one constant in our lives who will guide and watch over us no matter where we are or who we become. The legacy of motherhood is not a burden to her child—it's a gift. Through all the ups and downs, the trying moments and happy resolutions, our mothers exude pride in our maturity. Our mothers hold us near and dear to their hearts, just as we hold them in ours.

The Days of Camelot

By Pat Gallant

Dear Mom,

I remember our days in the White House, the first time I saw that senator from Massachusetts. Aside from the Beatles, he had the longest hair I'd ever seen on a man. When he began talking politics, I actually paid attention. He was a politician who was bright, young, handsome, witty, and dare I say—interesting. And that voice. . . .

I began tuning into the news, hoping to catch a glimpse of him as he sought the Democratic nomination for president. And finally, when John F. Kennedy won the Democratic ticket, I sat glued to the news. On one such occasion, Senator Kennedy appeared on television. Standing beside him was you—my own mother. YOU?

I was shocked. I looked hard at the television, rubbing my eyes to get better focus. Yet there you were, and when he finished talking, he put his arm around your waist and you both walked off. Quickly, I made a beeline to your bedroom to be sure you were here at home—in New York City—in our white apartment building. And you were. I yelled out excitedly about what I'd just seen, but you only half-listened as I insisted that, whoever this woman was, she was your double.

It took a few weeks before Kennedy made another appearance, but I was looking out for it. This time the lady was identified as Jacqueline Bouvier Kennedy, wife of Senator John F. Kennedy. I charged into your room and turned on the television. You and Dad watched, transfixed. And then the phone started ringing off the hook. Apparently, I now had company in my perception. Your hairstyle was the same as Jackie Kennedy's. The mohair suits, handbags, and hats were the same. The way you both wrapped your silk scarves around your head in the rain was the same, as were the oversized sunglasses. It was uncanny.

Finally, after Kennedy's many debates with the jowly Richard Nixon, it was announced that Kennedy had won. We had a new president, and now you were First Lady, which you always had been to us, anyway. But it wasn't until Kennedy took office and he and Mrs. Kennedy became constantly and highly visible that our lives shifted gears.

It first began when we'd taken a taxi to go shopping together at Bonwit Teller's. When we emerged from the taxi, you and I in our large sunglasses, I suddenly felt eyes upon us. People were pointing excitedly, nudging one another, and pulling each other towards us. I heard hushed voices and whispering. Finally, someone approached you with a pen and paper: "Can I have your autograph, Mrs. Kennedy?"

We were astonished. When you attempted to tell people you weren't Mrs. Kennedy, they walked away annoyed, positive that you were snubbing or tricking them to avoid signing autographs. People absolutely refused to believe you, and would insist on at least a handshake. You obliged them, Mom, but I was less scrupulous. I used to beg you to sign Mrs. Kennedy's name, but you wouldn't do it.

Everywhere we went, we drew looks, whispers, and sometimes even crowds. This became routine. At the time, you didn't realize that I played a little game. I'd fall a few paces behind you so it would appear you were alone, because, after all, if you were Mrs. Kennedy, who was I? Then I'd watch. I got a real kick out of that.

Though he was slow to admit it, Dad was beginning to enjoy your notoriety, too. Before this you had been, as he liked to say, the "boutonniere on his lapel" when you walked down the street together. Now, perhaps you were the president's boutonniere, as well.

The fun lasted until Kennedy was shot, and a whole society, a whole point in time, deflated. Everyone put away their Vaughn Meader albums, and watching Mrs. Kennedy became a sad reminder instead of a joy. Seeing Mrs. Kennedy mourn was even more difficult for me. It was like seeing you mourn.

One year later you got very sick. The beautiful, bright glow that emanated from you was fading before my eyes. Our lunch dates and shopping dates were over. Our long talks were slipping from us. My best friend in the world was dying.

Somewhere near the end, I found you crying. You hadn't done that through your entire illness, at least not in front of me. You looked up at me, telling me the Christmas gift you'd ordered for me hadn't come, that the entire order had been lost and would never arrive in time for Christmas. I couldn't believe my ears. You had thought of me when you were so weak, so near death, and you were crying not for yourself, but for me. We held each other very tightly for a long, long time, and I sensed I would have to remember that hug, because I knew it would have to carry me for the rest of my life.

I will always remember those days, Mommy. Those days of late-night mother-daughter talks. Those days of having a president who was an idol. Those days of sharing the limelight with Jackie Kennedy. Those days of unconditional love. Those days of having a mother. Our days. Our days in the White House. They were called the days of Camelot.

I LOVE YOU,

Pat
New York, New York

Writer Pat Gallant is a fourth-generation New Yorker, and mother of a son. She dedicates this letter to her mother, Gladys Selverne Gallant, whose book, Living Image, *was published posthumously by Doubleday and Co. in 1978.*

Strangers on a Train

BY GIGI PISORS

Dear Mom,

To many people, a book is something you simply pick up and read and then toss away. To me, a book meant life—a life filled with wondrous people, places, experiences, laughter, and above all, unconditional love. You literally found me in a book, a picture book that displayed the faces of more than 500 children who were, as yet, unclaimed by society. You saw me in that book. And you chose me.

I was six years old when my biological mother passed away. Until age twelve I was housed in eight different foster homes, most of which could be considered acceptable. I was one of the fortunate ones. But despite my favorable foster situation, I remained, as most orphan children do, overwhelmed by the longing to have a family of my own. Images of living in a house with loving, caring parents and perhaps even siblings permeated my dreams—especially when I was twelve and still in the "system," as it is termed. At that age you sometimes lose hope of ever getting adopted, and your faith diminishes with each passing year.

In the early seventies, the need for adoptive parents was more widely advertised. At that time, pictures of children were posted on the side of trains in the hope of gaining more exposure. I was one of those unclaimed children. At the same time, our pictures were also compiled into a book, and that is how you found me.

You were a single woman, and at that time it was very rare that nonmarried women adopted children. You had to endure extensive background checks and physical testing. The fact that you had attended school in a convent perhaps gave you an edge. After all, with God on your side, how could you go wrong?

You prevailed, and much to my delight, I became your daughter in 1978. The first day I met you at the adoption agency you gave me a special clear-covered folder with pictures of the house we would live in, the animals you had, and your yellow Toyota that always stalled in the rain. We sure had fun pushing that car! The folder also included pictures of the family I would become part of—wonderful grandparents, a trio of aunts, and two uncles. The two people I immediately warmed up to were my grandfather, whom I adored and who spoiled me rotten, and my grandmother, who welcomed me with open arms.

One of the most touching memories I have of becoming part of this wonderful family you brought me into was when the adoption was finalized and we went to Grandma and Grandpa's house for the first time. It was there that you had twenty-four presents waiting for me. A dozen for each birthday you'd missed, and a dozen more for each Christmas.

Mom, on more than one occasion I've asked you what made you pick me from a book that displayed so many hopeful faces. You said you were drawn to me and knew right away that I belonged with you. The funny thing is that so many people we came to know over the years couldn't believe I was adopted because you and I look so much alike.

I feel very blessed and lucky to have been chosen all those years ago, because there were many kids my age who weren't so fortunate. The unconditional love that you and the entire family showered upon me was magical. If it weren't for you my life would have turned out much differently.

I know we've had a few tough years, and I've had to learn a lot about trust and allowing people to love me. You are by far the most loving and selfless person I know. I honor the courage and willingness you had in taking a chance on an older child who was already set in her ways. From the bottom of my heart I thank you for everything, Mom. Most of all, for giving me a second chance at life, and for never giving up on me.

LOVE,

Gigi
Henderson, Nevada

Gigi Pisors is a pharmacy technician who lives in Henderson, Nevada, with her ten-year-old daughter, Briana. She enjoys scrapbooking, playing tennis, shopping, and spending quality time with her daughter.

Finding Mom in a Penny

BY TERESA C. VRATIL

Dear Mom,

I was looking for you for a long time. Although in the real world I knew that you had died, in my heart I was still looking for you. I just couldn't believe you were gone from my life forever. Whenever something exciting happened to me, I still picked up the phone to call you, not realizing until the phone rang that you wouldn't be answering. Your other children began to tell me that it was time—time for me to get used to a life without you.

But, I couldn't. I didn't want to lose you.

After many months of living in denial, I decided to take a trip to your favorite place in the Rocky Mountains. I didn't analyze my vacation choice; I just picked up the phone, booked a cabin, packed the car, and started driving. It was hard without you by my side, singing along with the radio or talking, but I heard a voice deep in my heart that told me this was the right thing to do.

I arrived at my cold, dark cabin too tired to look for you, so I climbed into bed and cried myself to sleep. The next morning, I made a plan to visit all the places that reminded me of you. My first stop was the campsite we visited for two weeks every summer throughout my childhood. I inhaled the sweet smell of pine, remembering those summers, which only made me realize I would never again share a campsite with you. As I kicked the coals from another family's abandoned campfire, I uncovered a penny, and without thinking, put it in my pocket.

Next I made my way to the river. As I walked the trail, I remembered the many times I followed you as you struggled with a book in one hand and in the other, an oversized lawn chair that banged against your leg with every step. When I reached the clearing at the edge of the river, instead of finding the sense of peace I was longing for, I only felt the loss of you from my life. As my head dropped to my chest in despair, I spotted another penny.

The next few days I continued to look for you in all our favorite places. I never found you, but I always found a penny. As I was packing up my suitcase on the last day of the trip, I picked up the pile of pennies I'd collected along the way. A voice—your voice—told me that you'd never really left me, that you'd be by my side always, and you were sending me those pennies as a reminder.

After that trip I found pennies everywhere I went. Stepping out of my car, grocery shopping, even in the emergency room when my son had an appendectomy. I grew to expect the coins, and looked forward to finding them when I wanted or needed you close.

Recently, I was very excited to be moving into my first home, but was feeling especially sad that you weren't with me to share the experience. Each day as I was preparing the new house, I tore down old wallpaper and ripped up shag carpeting, expecting to find your penny, but I went weeks without finding one. Again, I began to feel that you'd abandoned me, that I was alone. The night before the moving van arrived with all my furniture, I swept the entire house, expecting that I would find that one penny from you—but there was nothing.

The next morning I arrived at my new home with the movers in tow. I had trouble opening the door; my arms loaded with items. I stumbled over the threshold and dropped my keys, and as I bent to pick them up off my freshly swept floors, I discovered a shiny new penny.

Mom, I still find your pennies, but I don't need them to remember that you are with me always. You are in the eyes of my son and the smiles of my brothers. You are in my heart and always will be.

LOVE,

T

Tecumseh, Kansas

Teresa C. Vratil lives and writes in Leawood, Kansas, with her husband, John, and her seventy-pound canine "baby," Lola. She has been published in the Kansas City Star *and* Heavenly Patchwork.

Recipe for Life

BY JOAN HOBERNICHT

Dear Mom,

Today my daughter Jayna telephoned to ask for your sweet-potato casserole recipe, so I took my pink folder out of the pantry, and there in the back of the slim cookbook was the well-worn index card. Your handwriting was shaky when you wrote out the recipe at least thirty years ago. I thought I heard you sigh when I closed the pantry door, and I suddenly felt close to you, even though you've been gone sixteen years.

Cooking didn't interest either one of us, but that recipe never failed. Sometimes on holidays you would stay the night with us and make the casserole for our family dinner. Everyone loved it and asked for the recipe. Even now that casserole gets compliments when I contribute it to the potlucks I occasionally attend. The last time I used it was at Christmas when we were invited to a potluck at the home of friends here in Havasu. One guest commented that he never cared much for sweet potatoes, but he sure enjoyed that casserole!

Like your casserole, you always left a lasting impression, Mom. During your lifetime, teaching was your calling, and you were always looking for ways to improve your methods and to motivate and inspire your students. The years you spent teaching special education enriched many lives. Your students loved you and remember you to this day. For a while, I followed in your footsteps as a teacher, but my heart wasn't in it. Then I lost myself in the family grocery business.

Growing up, my mind was always focused on fiction. Being the third daughter in the family, I often felt unnecessary and would sit on the porch and make up stories, knowing that some day I would write novels. One time you sat beside me and asked me what I was thinking. I wouldn't tell you because I was afraid you'd think I was silly to have such lofty ideas. Now I wish I'd confided in you, as I'm certain you would've encouraged me in my ambition.

Nowadays, I am pursuing my dream of writing fiction. Many of the things you told me about our family have found their way into my stories, and those memories come to me now as I hold your recipe in my hands.

I'm so happy that Jayna plans to carry on the tradition of your casserole as a third-generation cook. Jesse is her second son, and he is now married. Perhaps his wife, Tiffany, will someday ask for the recipe too.

Sweet Potato Casserole

1 large can of sweet potatoes, drained and mashed
1 regular size can of crushed pineapple, drained
½ cup of dark brown sugar
2 large eggs, lightly whipped
Crushed walnuts to taste
1 package of marshmallows or marshmallow bits

Mix all ingredients together except the marshmallows and pour into medium-sized buttered casserole dish. Bake thirty minutes in pre-heated oven set at 375°F. Add marshmallows and bake five more minutes.

I was going to type the recipe onto my computer, but I've changed my mind. I'll write it on an index card in my arthritic handwriting in the hope that someday, after I'm long gone, Jayna will look at it and remember me, just as I have remembered you today.

LOVE,

Joan
Lake Havasu City, Arizona

Joan Hobernicht is married with four grown children and ten grandchildren. She is active in local writing groups and enjoys reading and helping her husband with his flea market booth.

IOU

By Esme Mills

Dear Mum,

I'll bet when I finished high school and moved out into my first apartment (even if it only lasted six weeks), you probably thought that your financial responsibility toward me had ended, except, of course, for my birthday and other special events. So you're probably scratching your head and wondering why—fifteen years later—you're still acting as my own personal bank.

It's not exactly what I had in mind either. I had kind of imagined being married, having two kids, and enjoying a six-figure bank account. At least I got the two kids. One out of three ain't bad.

For the record, I definitely don't want you to think that I don't appreciate your help or that I take it for granted. Just so we're clear, I've written up an IOU:

$4,500 for tuition when I wanted to be a travel agent.

$13,000 for tuition when I wanted to be a computer programmer.

$1,375 for tuition when I just wanted to be.

$2,894 for meals, including restaurants, Sunday brunches, and even leftovers that I took from your fridge because I had nothing better to eat at my place. (I'll try to bring the plastic containers back soon.)

$2,369 for the time I needed to get out of a bad relationship and you hired the movers.

$5,550 that I saved on a private hospital room by having a home birth at your house, in that fabulous room with a Jacuzzi, overlooking the ocean. What a wonderful way to welcome my son to the world! (Actually, double that amount, given that the other one came along two years later.)

$1,485 that I would have paid babysitters who canceled at the last minute, but then you saved the day or night.

$241 for chocolate in times of need.

$12,750 for actual loans that you probably don't actually expect to collect on.

Grand total: $49,714

I'm just wondering if you would possibly accept a lifetime supply of hugs and kisses in lieu of cash?

IOU,

Esme

Pender Island, British Columbia, Canada

Esme Mills lives on Pender Island, British Columbia, with her mother and two boys. She thanks her mother for believing in her dream to write and helping to make it a reality.

The Yellow Notebook

BY ANDREA NORVILLE

Dear Mom,

I was in your closet the other day, rummaging for old tax forms. Apparently, you've kept every single important document that chronicles the history of our entire family. Amid the medical records, report cards, and old birthday cards, I found a dusty and faded yellow notebook, like the ones I used in school. I opened it up and saw the date at the top of the page: *April 10, 1989.*

You kept a journal and I never knew about it. You wrote that you wanted to start a journal because you felt "time slipping by." I was only seven years old, and my brother Eric was three. We were in the middle of moving to our house on Howard Street. You seemed very optimistic about the new house, even though it was more than 200 years old; had dripping faucets and leaking ceilings; and desperately needed new carpeting and wallpaper.

I remember the first day you brought us to the house. It looked like the grass hadn't been cut in months, and the grass was almost as tall as I was. I'm sure when you looked at it, all you could see was another daunting task to accomplish, but I remember thinking that being able to hide in the tall grass was the best thing about the house.

In your journal you wrote down all of the funny things Eric and I said day-to-day, such as, "You my best mudder," and in the springtime "I didn't know the leaves turn green again!" You described in great detail all of the little outings we took, the restaurants we ate at, the parks we played in, and the parties we had. We were always with friends or family. You made sure we had so many memorable experiences as little children.

I also see now how much you worried about us. You worried about how sensitive I was at such a young age. You wrote that I once came home from school concerned about Ivory soap. I had drawn a picture of an elephant holding up a "No Ivory Soap" sign. I must have been confused!

You wrote that after I had a bad case of the chicken pox you tried to make me more comfortable with a baking-soda bath. While you were putting lotion on me I said, "What would I do without a mother?" It seems it was easier to say those kinds of things when I was seven years old, but even now I don't know what I would do without you.

Dad had just started working nights, and you were with us all day. Eric was a bit fussier than I had been at his age, and even though I didn't notice at the time, I now see how hard it was to keep things under control. But no matter how stressful it got, you only wrote about the fun we had that day and how proud of us you were. You wanted the best for us, which is why we moved to Howard Street in the first place. We had more space to play outside, and it was a quiet, safe neighborhood.

It's been seventeen years since you stopped writing. I am now twenty-four, and in the process of buying my own home. Soon, we will all be moving out of our historical colonial on Howard Street, and from all of those memories that are written in your journal. I just thought you should know, Mom, that I'm taking the yellow notebook with me to continue your tradition.

LOVE ALWAYS,

Andrea

North Providence, Rhode Island

Andrea Norville was born and raised in Massachusetts. She graduated from Bridgewater State College in 2005 with a bachelor's degree in English. She now works in publishing and recently bought her first house in Rhode Island.

Scent from Heaven

BY JOANN RENO WRAY

Dear Mom,

I still long to talk to you on the phone, even though it's
been thirteen years since you graduated to heaven. It
doesn't seem fair that you left us at the young age of
sixty-four, when the two of us had just begun a great
friendship, and were at last truly blending as mother and
daughter.

All those wasted years as I grew up. The anger. The
fear. The rejection. The verbal abuse. Most of all, the
lack of ever saying the words I ached to hear: "I love
you."

All that changed in 1979 when Roger and I were
about to move 900 miles away to another state. I'll
always remember how you followed me to the van
that day. Twisting your fingers together nervously,
you wouldn't stop talking, but said nothing. All the
while you dared not look at me until I moved closer
and noticed the sheen of tears in your eyes. "Mom,
what is it?" I asked, truly concerned. You never cried
easily.

You stepped closer, shocking me further by putting
your worn hands on my shoulders. You looked up briefly,
straight into my eyes. With a quivering voice you said, "I
don't want you to go. I love you so much!" I was thirty

years old, and for the first time I heard you speak those precious words, your smile beaming on me through the tears.

Five years ago, I visited my daughter Amie. She and her husband Joe had been trying so hard to have a baby. Then, over five months pregnant, she called one night from her Minnesota home hundreds of miles away. Screams and sobs greeted me when I answered the phone. She cried out to me for help. "Mommy, I'm bleeding! It hurts! The baby! Oh, no! Pray, Mommy!" I prayed with every cell in my body, thinking the entire time that what I was feeling was how you felt when I was so far from you and had my own troubles.

I went to Amie, to help and offer encouragement as any mother would. Mom, I knew you'd be there too in many ways—more than I realized at first. I arrived with plans for shopping and sightseeing, anything to take Amie's mind off the miscarriage. Instead, with the anniversary of your birth and death just days away, I was overwhelmed with melancholy, longing for you to be there with us.

How I longed for you at that moment. I knew you'd offer homespun wisdom, whip up a country meal, or just sit on the porch rocking along as we sat nearby. How could I ever offer adequate comfort to Amie when I could barely restrain my own tears?

The first morning at Amie's home, I realized I'd left home without my face powder, and you know that oversight almost constitutes a national disaster for me. Her community is so small that the closest stores were forty minutes away. "Amie," I asked with little hope, since she rarely wore cosmetics, "do you have any face powder I can borrow?"

To my surprise, she rummaged around in the cabinets and pulled out a small round container of face powder imprinted with white powder puffs on a gold and black background. I turned it over in my hands, then placed it on the table. It was vaguely familiar.

Amie looked concerned. "Are you okay, Mom? That powder was in the box of things I brought back from Grandma Reno's after her funeral. I don't use it. You might as well take it."

I stared at the now familiar container, over- whelmed by memories of you getting "gussied up" for a family reunion or a rare evening out with Dad. After a few minutes, I opened it. Mom, that sweet powdery scent painted your smiling face vividly before me. You rarely wore perfume, but that face powder was your constant and only adornment, aside from lipstick.

I brought that powder home with me, and I now wear the same brand. When I open that round box and catch a whiff of the sweet powdery scent, you're with me in an instant, Mom. I gaze in the mirror and powder my nose, but what I really see is you standing next to me, smiling back with that same smile of approval God finally granted me from your heart when I was thirty years old. Thanks for that scent from heaven, and the reminder that you still love me.

JoAnn
Broken Arrow, Oklahoma

JoAnn Reno Wray lives near Tulsa, Oklahoma, with her husband, Roger. Since 1974, her writing/graphic arts business, EpistleWorks Creations (http://epistleworks.com), has brought hope and healing through words and images.

A Love Entwined

By Tel Asiado

Dear Mama,

Lately, I've been thinking of you with a sense of nostalgia, and when I do, I think of courage, kindness and a loving heart—virtues that manifested themselves in every aspect of your life. A devoted wife and mother, you were meticulous with orderliness and cleanliness, and saw to it that everything was organized in our home.

I grew up in a local town with our close-knit family of Christian believers. Our family life revolved around church-related activities, with you and Papa deeply committed to God and obedient to Christ's teachings. Our home was always open to relatives, friends, and fellow believers. Until I was in high school, some cousins and one of your kind elderly relatives lived with us. After dinner, we would usually sing, and oftentimes, in the comfort of a quiet twilight, you picked up your classical guitar and played. One piece of music I particularly remember is *Lagrima* by Tarrega. Your music was so beautiful, Mama. There is so much music, so much joy when there's love at home.

You and Papa hardly left my bedside when I was ill. Being an only child, I was overprotected and devoid of freedom that ordinary children enjoyed. I resented this exceedingly at that time, but despite it, you both strictly adhered to "spare the rod and spoil the child."

I must have been five or six when you saw to it that I began taking piano lessons. When I started school, you were there holding my hand. You sewed me beautiful dresses almost every week, the envy of other children. You were always there for me throughout my high school years, and when I discovered boys in those teenage years, you were strict but understanding as I entertained the excitement and anxieties of young love.

Every time I was hurting, you were there to ease my pain, Mama. Through joy and tears, you shared my triumphs and disappointments, and you were always proud of me. When I earned academic awards and recognition, you were happy and beaming with humble pride.

The most difficult decision you made with Papa was for me to leave you, to move to the big city to attend university. Like most parents, you could've opted that I study at the local college. Instead, you sought the best for my advancement and growth in pursuit of higher learning. That was the beginning of my life away from you and the shelter of home. The trade-off was difficult for you, but for my sake you took the sacrifice at your own expense.

Across the distance, while I was in school, you continuously supported me financially and with your

love, but you kept silent about your deteriorating
health concerns, among other problems, so as not to
worry me. Ever thoughtful and humorous, your spirit
and will far surpassed anything I could feel from your
letters. It was almost too easy to forget just how
difficult yours and Papa's debilitating illnesses had
become. When I was still living at home, your health
troubles never fazed you, and you enjoyed independence
apart from your physical pain. When overwhelmed,
not once did you complain of pain or utter a sound
that gave evidence of your discomfort.

During my last visit home, I experienced a
premonition that it would be the last time I'd see you
alive. It was evident from the contained sadness in
your eyes. Yet, without fail, you managed the forever
impish and loving smile that so characterized you.

Mama, for some time now, I've been in my worst
crises, including career and financial difficulties. In all
this, I've derived strength from the courage and faith
you taught and showed me. Pressed to the limits with
no options left, I've been drawn to God by these
crises, and I'm humbled. As I wade through my
trying times, I think of you. I'm grateful for the
legacies you left behind—an unflinching faith in God,
a continuous thirst for learning, and kindness to
others.

You will never read this letter. You left this earth
two decades ago, and I left home a decade before that,
but I know my thoughts will get to you. By love, our

hearts and souls are entwined, and I will forever feel the bond that connects me to you.

ALL MY LOVE,

Tel

Sydney, Australia

Tel Asiado is an IT project manager turned writer, author, and consultant. She holds a degree in chemistry and an MBA in computer management. Her writings reflect a lifelong passion for motivational, Christian insights and classical music.

Too Cool for School

By Briana C. Ferrell

Dear Mom,

Thank you for everything and especially having me.
Another thing is for all the cool things you have bought
for me. Also for being the coolest Mom ever, unlike the
other Moms in my class. Your the best Mom ever and I
would never replace you. I just wanted to let you know
that you are the most joyful, helpful, fun and
understanding Mom ever.

Mom, I may not tell you how much I appreciate
and Love you very often, but I am now.

HUGS AND KISSES,

Briana

Henderson, Nevada

*Ten-year-old Briana
Ferrell lives in
Henderson, Nevada.
She loves to play tennis,
write stories, read, and go swimming, especially during the hot
summers. She also enjoys playing with her pet bunny, Bix.*

Getting to Know You

BY LINDA BRUNO

Dearest Momma,

I've always been the one to ask questions, haven't I?
Over the last twelve months, so many questions have
flooded my mind at the strangest times. Questions I
have never dared ask.

As I read about relationships, I want to ask—what
attracted you to Dad when you were just sixteen, and
he was a worldly twenty-one-year-old ex-Marine? How
did you feel when you found yourself expecting a child
at such a young age? Were you happy? Sad? Angry?
Did you ever wonder if marrying him was the right
choice?

As I read about older women who are reinventing
themselves and pursuing new dreams, I wonder—what
were your dreams? Was there a career you yearned for?
A place you always wanted to live?

As my husband and I grow older, I wonder how
you felt caring for a terminally ill spouse, especially
when you were so young and your health was so
fragile. Did you wonder, again, if you had made the
right choice so many years before? And after he died,
did you miss him, or did you honestly feel as if you'd
been set free?

Over the years you and I eventually found ourselves in unfamiliar and uncomfortable roles. You became dependent on your kids for support—sometimes financial, and always emotional—and I tried to help while pretending you didn't really need it. And even though we spent a lot of time together, I never found a way to ask you some of the hard questions surrounding your fears, your joys, and your frustrations. Our conversations avoided the deeper discussions that would have allowed me to know you better.

I told you I loved you every time we talked, and you always answered in kind, sometimes even saying it first. And although we didn't divulge our deepest feelings, we tried to express them in other ways. One of the things I cherish in life are the birthday cards you gave me, two of which I still carry with me in my Bible. In those cards you always wrote your feelings, though I'm not sure you realized how much your words truly meant to me when you wrote: *"Dearest Daughter, Just as this card says, you are truly a blessing. A Momma could ask for nothing more."*

You may not have expressed your feelings verbally, but now I have them to hold in my hands, to take out and read when I need to feel you close in my heart.

As your health deteriorated, my need to ask questions became crucial, except now I was asking those questions of healthcare professionals. Would you ever be able to overcome the frailty that resulted from weighing a mere seventy pounds? Were there programs available that would allow you to stay in your home with some semblance of the semi-independence you cherished?

The issues we faced were terribly important, but we danced around what was really happening, never mentioning the fate that hovered over us like a dark cloud. When hospice became a part of our lives, you resisted until I lovingly explained to you that they would do whatever you wanted them to do. Without acknowledging what was facing us, I tearfully whispered, "I can't fix this." And you understood.

Now it was your turn to ask questions. Not the deep, philosophical questions I once longed for, but simple, very important questions. You wanted to know, "Will they make me take that vitamin pill? It's so hard to swallow." *No, Momma, they won't make you take that pill.* "Will they stick my finger twice a day to test my sugar? My skin hurts so much." *No, Momma, we aren't going to worry about your sugar anymore.* "Will they make me eat? I don't want to eat." *No, Momma, you don't have to eat if you don't want to.*

Then it was my turn to ask you one of the most important questions I've ever asked. "Momma, what can I do for you?"

And you said, very softly, "Just be here for me." And I was, Momma, I was.

At 4:35 A.M., on April 7, 2005, I was holding your hand as you took your last breath. The last words you heard were, "I love you, Momma," and it was at that instant that I realized nothing else really mattered. No questions, no philosophical, soul-searching discussions. Just "I love you, Momma." And I do.

ALWAYS,

Lindy
Ocala, Florida

Linda Bruno is a freelance writer, public speaker, and trainer. She is currently working on a devotional entitled All God's Creatures *and can be reached at lfbruno@cfl.rr.com.*

The Farm

By Karen L. Hudson

Mother Dear,

My daughters always ask me to tell them stories of when I was a kid, and it seems that when they put me on the spot I can't seem to think of anything really interesting. I mean, they all know I was raised on a farm and we had lots of animals and a big garden. Except for a lot of hard work, what else is there to tell?

I resented that farm. I didn't like getting dirty in the garden. I didn't like the smell of the pigs. I didn't like bugs attacking me in swarms as I walked to the barn. I didn't like having to miss out on Saturday-morning cartoons because there was work to do. But now I look back on the farm with a less judgmental eye. When I sit back and think about it, that farm made me the person I am today, and working with you on some of the most mundane chores are the memories I cherish the most.

The garden taught me that with hard work and sweat (and a lot of bitching and moaning), you will see the fruits of your labors. One year we planted gladiolas, and that was one of my proudest moments. We created 500 beautiful flowers, and we did it together. Today I'm not afraid of hard work, even if I won't see the results until much later.

The pigs taught me that even the worst messes—yes, Mom, even my bedroom—could be cleaned up. With some shoveling and fresh sawdust, those pigs came out smelling just fine. As such, I knew that when my life had fallen into a financial and social mess, I knew it could be cleaned up. The little oinkers also taught me not to judge people too harshly, because those funky pigs were very kind on the inside.

The bugs taught me . . . well, they taught me to use bug spray.

I loved freezing corn with you. It was fun sneaking a chunk of kernels that were all stuck together when we sliced them off the cob. I enjoyed those times we sat together in the screen-house and snapped peas and beans. I can still hear the popping sound they made. I remember drying fruit, and excitedly checking the dehydrator to see if the dried fruit slices were ready. I'd put my face against the side of the dehydrator because a soft breeze came out of it and tickled my nose. I loved watching you water the plants in the house, when the watering can would make that funny glug as you tipped it back up.

The rest of the animals at the farm were actually pretty cool, too. On a cold day, nothing felt better than putting my hand under a warm chicken to collect its eggs. And we had a lot of laughs over goat antics. I was very proud of my beautiful bunny rabbit, even when those mean old 4-H judges said he was too fat. And I really did love the cats, even though you caught me swinging one around by its legs one day. I swear, Mom, Kitty and I were just dancing!

Living on the farm, I also learned the difficult lessons of life and death. That's not a fun lesson to learn at any age, but it forced me to acknowledge how precious life is, and to this day I believe fully in making the most of every moment. It's what has taught me to value family and friendship and to appreciate everything life has to offer, even the mundane chores and the hard lessons. I've learned not to sweat the small stuff.

So maybe that old farm wasn't so bad after all. You'll be happy to know that I've even developed a small interest in gardening and have been planting flowers in my own yard. But they'll never be as beautiful as those gladiolas we planted together, because it's you—not the flowers—that makes that memory so special.

Thanks, Mom. Now I know exactly what to tell my girls the next time they ask for a story.

Karen Lee
Indianapolis, Indiana

Karen L. Hudson has been married for thirteen wonderful years and is the proud mother of two beautiful daughters. For seven years she's been a guide for About.com, and is the editor of Chick Ink *(Adams Media).*

Heaven and Earth

By Garnet Miller

Dear Mom,

When I came home for Easter, I browsed through old photos of us kids. Most of our clothes were made on your old sewing machine, which sat next to Grandma's in her bedroom. I saw pictures of smiling brown faces dressed head-to-toe in matching outfits imprinted with Hanna-Barbera characters. You sure knew how to stretch a buck.

You once told me that all you ever wanted to be was a mother. I have come to realize that you were the one constant in my life. You sacrificed your wants and dreams time and time again for me and my sisters. I couldn't see it then, but I've since learned how children have that effect on the parents who love them.

Until a few years ago, I thought all I would ever be able to focus on were the bad memories of my childhood. My whole world turned on its ear when Dad walked out. At once, comfort and security were displaced by fear and anger. At eight years of age, I was too young to see that you felt the same way. I blamed you because you didn't try to stop him from leaving.

As a result of Dad's departure, you had to rejoin the workforce for the first time since taking your vows. You needed not one, but two jobs to support our family.

Still, you made breakfast in the morning and dinner in the evening. Maintaining a semblance of normalcy for your children was important to you.

I don't remember you questioning me when I told you in my most grown-up eleven-year-old voice that I wanted to go live with Dad. You only said, "If that's what you want to do, baby." So you watched Dad take me to the lawyer's office. The lawyer asked me if I truly wanted to live with my father, and in my anger, I said, "Yes." You then watched as Dad took me to visit what would be my new school, and you stood by the door when he picked me up for my first official night in my new residence.

How it must have shattered your heart to wave good-bye and see me go. You had lost your husband *and* your daughter. What you would soon know was that I had the worst night of my life when I left you that day. I had stayed with Dad before for weekend visits so I figured my new arrangement would be a piece of cake. Not so.

For the first time, I slept in a bedroom without my sisters, and knowing that no one was coming to pick me up on Sunday scared me to death. My weeping and wailing brought Dad running into the room. Between sobs, I managed to mumble "Mom" and "go home." My sobbing didn't cease until he pulled up in front of our apartment and I fell into your waiting arms. I couldn't last a single night without you.

Today, the second of May, I celebrate my fourteenth wedding anniversary, and what a wild ride it has been.

Things in our marriage were less than ideal at first, as I'd gleaned the wrong impression from your life. I kept my heart distant from my husband and the boys because I feared being hurt like Dad and I hurt you. But when my marriage threatened to fall apart, God helped me see the true example of your life. Love had not become a curse to you; instead, it became strength. The love you showered on us sustained you as well, and when I realized that, it felt like the windows of heaven had been thrown open and I'd been given a second chance. God showed me that love shared with another is never a waste, no matter the outcome.

I love my family better today because you loved me best a long time ago. When folks tell you how beautiful and talented your three daughters have become, you humbly say, "I hope I had a little to do with it." Well baby, God gave you the gift of mothering and it has made all the difference in the world to me—just ask your grandkids.

Love,

Garnet

Greensboro, North Carolina

Garnet Miller is a freelance writer and member of FaithWriters.com. She resides in Greensboro, North Carolina, with her husband, David, and two young sons.

Fanesia

BY ANNE SKALITZA

Dear Mom,

I sit in a blue plastic chair, my back straight, yet my body leaning slightly toward the metal rail of your hospital bed in the Intensive Care Unit. I raise my hand and hesitantly touch your hand as a single tear creeps down my face, unnoticed. I lightly run my hand over the hospital bracelet that bears your name— Frances.

It seems like there are a thousand tubes twisting away from your prone body toward machines that beep their coded messages to the nurses, and hiss like snakes ready to pounce on the first visitor who dares intrude on their space. I slip my hand through yours and almost imperceptibly your thumb rubs over mine in a comforting gesture of love—the only response that can be elicited. I whisper, "I love you" to you, who until three days ago walked faster than I, and insisted that going up and down the stairs in your own home was the best way to exercise. Unfortunately, those very stairs proved to be your undoing, and I'll look upon them now with horror, as I remember you lying on the polished wood floor at the base of the stairway.

Sitting quietly by your bedside, I have much time to contemplate and pray. Without fail, my mind plays like an old movie reel, spliced too many times, displaying bits and pieces of your life as told to me throughout my childhood and adulthood.

"The road and I, we traveled together," you would say whenever you related a story about your past. It wasn't that you were a well-traveled person; rather the message was metaphorical. More often than not, your road was full of potholes. But despite the twists and turns and rough shoulders, you stayed on that road and held steadfast to your journey. It was always your goal to do the best you could with whatever lay in your path.

It was on a rain-soaked day that you were born to Italian immigrants who didn't speak English. Baptized "Fanesia," your life journey began, but you said that no one probably took notice of your birth, since World War I was raging overseas. This was to be the tone of how you journeyed through life—unobtrusively but with purpose. With God at your side, you always felt reassurance that no matter what path you traveled, what bumps and potholes you encountered, you would be all right.

And now, as I, your youngest daughter, sit by your bedside listening to the whirs of the machines that sustain you, I know that the Lord is watching over you. I too, am reassured that even though the road you bravely traveled will surely end soon, your legacy of living life unobtrusively but with purpose, and knowing God is always with us, will travel on through your daughters and grandchildren.

WITH UNENDING LOVE,

Your Anne

Spring Lake, New Jersey

Anne Skalitza lives three blocks from the Atlantic Ocean with her husband, two sons, and her sister. A freelance writer, she works from her home office, where she hears the shushing sound of the ocean and the cry of gulls.

Out for a Drive

BY JAMIE J. GILLIAM

Dear Mom,

There is much I want to tell you and so much I forgot to share. Time passes, and with each new memory created, there is that much more I need for you to know.

My daughters, the girly-girls, are much older now—seven, twelve, and fifteen. I see so much of me in each of them. In turn, I also see you. They are such incredible girls, but I still have absolutely no idea what I'm doing. There must be magic in this mix, because it appears that so far I'm doing something right. It's important to me that the girly-girls know you, know your story. We miss you, and in those moments we're missing you, we know that you're here with us.

I honor you by sharing your life, wisdom, and spirit. The girly-girls can describe with the most vivid detail the memories of my past. The carefree days spent on a boat, holidays, an island with little monkeys greeting us, baking on Saturday mornings, the world's worst strawberry milk, and the photos. The photographs really help. Without them, the task of describing my life would be significantly more difficult. In them are glimpses of an extremely shy child who is obscured by corners, the pleats in your skirts, the shadows in which I hid. The photographs help me remember some of what I could not otherwise see clearly.

Each of the girly-girls can tell these stories as if they were their own. Remember your very first car? It was a shiny new Toyota wagon parked in the driveway. It's one of my very fondest memories. I loved the times when you'd load my sister Aly and me into the wagon to "go for a drive." I don't know if it was five or fifteen minutes with the three of us sitting there in the driveway, but it was simply fun. Each time you would get out with the biggest smile emanating from your entire being and ask, "Now, wasn't that a fun drive?"

I will always look back on those drives as being the very best. We never actually went anywhere. Heck, you never even started the car. But in hindsight, it's still terribly funny. You owned a car that you didn't know how to drive, and no one knew except for your twin girls who really didn't care.

Did I tell you I have a photograph of you on my dresser? It's of your wedding day. In it I see where I get my big smiles, small ankles, and body shape. It's comforting. I see me in you.

Can you see me?

Can you hear me?

I've gotten so much older. Would you recognize me if you saw me, recognize my heart, the essence of who I am? I hope so. I am much like you and I live the lessons you taught so many years ago: laugh, love fully, tell it like it is, give and then give even more, celebrate the small things in life, make good choices, pineapple upside-down cake heals "owies," and long drives in a parked car are worthwhile trips.

I keep forgetting to tell you something I have recently read. I think of it often: *Forgiveness is the act of letting go of the belief that the past should be different.* This has become my life's challenge. I struggle with forgiving you.

To forgive you would be to somehow believe that your leaving me was okay. I wish the past were different. I wish I had known to say good-bye. I wish seven-year-olds would never have to discover how very far away heaven is. I wish you were here with me and that sometimes I could still hide—if only for a moment—in the safety of your arms or behind your skirts. I can't, so I'll continue to be the safe haven for my girlies, continue to be brave, face the world, smile, talk to you often, and continue to practice forgiveness until I master it.

Tonight I'm making pineapple upside-down cake with the girly-girls. Once again we'll talk about long drives in a parked car and a grandma they can only know through photographs and my voice.

I love you and I miss you beyond measure, and Aly sends her love too.

Your Jamie Jo
Oceanside, California

Jamie J. Gilliam resides in a small beach community in California, raising her three children. She serves as an office manager for TMI, a full-service investment real estate brokerage and management company, and as CEO for Advocacy in Action, Inc., a nonprofit company developed to benefit mentally disabled adults and children. She dedicates this letter to her mother, Patricia Gilliam.

5.

It's Never Too Late to Say Thank You

I n one form or another, we are all a reflection of our mothers and their teachings. They lead by example, and if we're smart, we learn to accept their gifts and carve our own destiny atop the firm foundation they've laid for us. We may not always see eye to eye, but in the grand scheme of things, that matters little. The memories that stay with us are evident each time we look in the mirror or close our eyes.

Our mothers teach us to dream, to hope, to live. They want the best for us and look forward to the day when they can share in our joy, knowing that all they worked so hard to teach us has brought us peace, contentment, and success. All children strive to please their mothers, but in truth, it is a mother who works hard to please a child. Whether subtle or stout, in times of abundance or hardship, a mother stands tall and resolute in her quest to provide the best possible life for her child.

To simply thank a mother seems incredibly inadequate. How do you thank someone for giving you life? For helping you read, tie your shoes, learn the alphabet, and for caring for you when you're in pain? There is no measure of words that can describe our true feelings for our mothers, save for the four words every mother hopes to hear: "I love you, Mom."

On Angels' Wings

BY BHASWATI GHOSH

Dearest Ma,

Do you remember that afternoon all those summers ago when you came to your five-year-old daughter's school at lunchtime? My class teacher had summoned you to share with you the alarming fact of my "dullness."

"She is really slow in catching up with the lessons, Mrs. G.," she warned you, adding, "I hope you will take the necessary steps at home. If she doesn't fare better, we will have to stop her promotion to the next class."

You listened to her in silence, never once getting confrontational. Only when she was done reporting her annoyance with me, did you politely say: "I appreciate your concern, Mrs. Kundu, but I refuse to accept that my daughter is dull. You don't have to take my word on that—she will prove it to you."

As the teacher smirked in disbelief and left the classroom in a huff to join her colleagues for lunch, your little one remained slumped in the corner, resting her head on the desk, waiting for a fairy to come and soothe her. How could I know you were that fairy, Ma?

As you made your way through the rows of seats to reach me, my classmates huddled around you, bellowing out the big news of the day. "Aunty, Aunty, do you know Bhaswati got a zero on today's test?"

"Yeah, Aunty, ma'am was very angry with her. She said she has never seen someone so dull."

"Bhaswati isn't talking to us, Aunty. She's upset because she got a zero."

The cacophony tore me apart, even more than the teacher's disgust. These were my friends, but instead of being by my side they were competing with each other to tell my mother about my pathetic test performance.

You just smiled at them and said gently, "Ah, so Bhaswati got a zero, did she?"

"Yeah, Aunty, yeah Aunty," the voices screeched again.

"Okay, let's see. Did any of you get a zero?"

"No, Aunty, no." The other girls loudly declared their results, and they had reason enough to be loud—none of them did worse than me.

"So none of you got a zero, right? Only Bhaswati did. Why are you all so worked up, then? Cheer up, children, go out and play. You should be happy you didn't get a zero, shouldn't you?"

Stupefied silence. All at once, you had checkmated the noisy gaggle of girls.

As they quietly walked out of the classroom with their lunchboxes, you came over to me. Without saying a word, you took me in your arms and started patting me softly on the back—the soft touch I'd known since birth. Then you wiped my tears and whispered. "Nothing has happened, *Mamoni*, nothing at all. Now cheer up, my sweet angel, show me a smile, quickly!" Despite my stiff resistance, you did extract a smile from me.

You didn't say a word to me about the test. You didn't ask why I could not manage to get even a single question correct. Instead, you sheltered me in your arms, like a mother bird would protect her fledglings. Then, you opened my lunchbox and fed me.

All these summers later, Ma, I haven't forgotten that afternoon and the little girl I was at the time. I realized that even when the entire world stood against me, I still had an anchor holding steady on the other side of the shore.

The incident happened just a few months before my final exams. You spent the next few weeks teaching your "dull and slow" daughter, and I loved every moment of it. You brought such vitality and joy to the learning.

When the final exams were over and the results were revealed, Mrs. Kundu had to bite the bullet. Our team—the resolute mother and the dull daughter—had proven her wrong. To everyone's shock, I had secured a place among the top ten students in the class.

Bless Mrs. Kundu's heart. She brought out the best in me, but more than that, she helped me see the angel my mother is.

LOVINGLY,

Pompa
New Delhi, India

Freelance writer Bhaswati Ghosh lives in New Delhi, India. Her book, Making Out in America, *is a humorous, anecdotal account of her experiences with American slang and colloquialisms. Her other interests include singing, cooking, and traveling. Her Web site is http://bghosh.cavernreal.com.*

Saving Grace

BY B.J. HALL

Dear Mom,

There are times when I sit and think about how wrong I have been to people, but especially to you, who struggled to cope with my selfish and self-destructive ways. I miss you and always will. How cruel I was, as I lived a demeaning life in the streets and engaged in all sorts of antisocial behavior. I continue to try to forgive myself, but the acts I've committed have scarred me deeply. I still cry my heart out because you passed on before seeing the changes I've made in my life.

I had become a criminal to survive. I would do anything and everything for money. I've done many things I'm not proud of. I was a thief and assaulted anyone who got in my way. You went through so much on my behalf, crying every night while I roamed the streets. I was a troubled child and grew up feeling unloved and unwanted, which I know now was far from the truth. I didn't know where to go for help. I couldn't find my way, so all I did was worry you.

Even when you were on your deathbed, I didn't understand that you were about to leave me. Your last thoughts were not of yourself, but only of me. You let me know that you loved me, regardless of the life I was leading. You loved me—not my actions—and your love was unconditional. You instilled in me the ability to distinguish right from wrong, but I disregarded your valuable life lessons. I barely made it to your funeral, showing up in dirty clothes, my hair unkempt, and smelling like a garbage can. I looked like the homeless person I was.

Today, I'm a grown man. I cry at times and wish you were here to see me now. I want to believe that you knew that I'd eventually change my life and become a decent individual. Many of your friends thought I would meet death early. Others thought I would simply commit suicide. I have to admit I thought about it.

If I could talk to you now, I'd tell you how sorry I am for breaking your heart, for hurting and embarrassing you. I would tell you I never blamed you for the wrong course I chose. I wish I could smell your scent, your hair. I wish you could hold me and hug me, something I was uncomfortable with when you were alive. I would love you to know, dear Mother, that I'm now the kind of person you wanted me to be—compassionate, kind, caring, and loving. I've asked my God for forgiveness and to help me forgive myself. Above all, I'd tell you the one thing I never told you when you were alive: "Mother, I love you."

LOVE,

B.J.

Atlanta, Georgia

B.J. Hall is an avid golfer who enjoys babysitting his grandchildren.

My First Mother

BY LAURA S. ANDERSEN

Dear Sandi,

Thirty-seven years ago, you gave birth to a healthy seven-pound baby girl. You never held her, you never saw her, and two days after her birth you signed the adoption papers that made her someone else's daughter. From that day on, you lived your life and wondered about hers, your soul possessed with patience throughout the long years, waiting and hoping that one day she might come looking for you.

Four years ago, I came looking—and I found you. Since then, I like to think we've both found a measure of peace. Not that all of it has been simple. That's too much to hope for in any relationship, but especially one as uncharted as this. In the end, I can only say that I would make the same decision to search for you in a heartbeat—those heartbeats that began when you carried within you a baby daughter whose welfare was more important to you than your own wishes. In gratitude for that, I want to share with you some of the reasons I'm grateful to be your daughter.

First, I'm grateful because you've made the process of reunion as easy as it could be. I've read stories about bitter women who kept secrets and wouldn't acknowledge their children, women who were desperately needy, and women who made the entire process a nightmare. Thank you for making it easy for me, and for so patiently waiting for me to be ready to find you.

Second, I'm grateful because I have a mother who not only supports my creative efforts, but also who understands them. You instinctively know both the pleasure and pain of trying to make art out of words.

Third, I'm grateful to have a mother who has lived a life of such ambition and success, a mother who is fiercely intelligent and even more fiercely determined. It took me a long time to admit my own ambitions—a word that had always seemed a little suspect to me. I'm glad to know I come by it honestly.

Fourth, I'm grateful that my children have one more grandmother in their life to love and learn from, that their hearts can be opened to the numerous diversities of family love.

Last, and most importantly, I'm grateful because you helped make me who I am. At times I've wondered what I would have been like if I'd have been born to my parents, just as I've wondered what I would have been like if I had been raised by you. The only conclusion I've reached is that I would be somehow different in either case.

I like who I am. I like the way I look and the way my mind works. I cherish my love of words and stories, and the way I laugh and move my hands when I talk. I would have lost so much of who I am if I had not been your daughter first. I loved you long before I met you. Thank you for being my mother.

LOVE,

Laura

Saratoga Springs, Utah

Laura Andersen's daily goal is to have the same number of children (four) and husbands (one) at bedtime as she had in the morning, and to write in every spare moment amid the joyous chaos of raising a family.

Always My Mommy

By Bethany Finney

Dear Mommy,

Thank you for always being there for me, when I'm sad or feeling lonely. Thank you for being happy for me when something exciting happens to me. Thank you for home schooling me. Thank you for showing me Jesus, and thank you for taking care of me and loving me.

I love you, even though I don't show it all the time. I LOVE YOU!!

Love,

Bethany

Avon Park, Florida

Twelve-year-old Bethany Finney lives in Florida, where she is homeschooled along with her three siblings. She likes biking; rollerblading; swimming; singing; reading; and hanging out with friends, family, and her youth group. Her work has appeared on http://kids.faithwriters.com.

The Beat Goes On
BY LESLIE TERKEL WAKE

Dear Mom,

Is it too late to say thank you?

You passed on nearly twenty-seven years ago, so writing this letter may not seem entirely sane. But you loved me unconditionally, even when you were so often shaking your head and sighing. You taught me hundreds of lessons, and had at least that many opinions about me, which you shared with a mixture of pleasure and impatience, pride and disappointment.

At times the silence between us stretched enough to fill a room, while other times we laughed so hard into the night that our laughter followed me even into my sleep. You wanted so much for me, Mom, and now that I am a mother of three teenaged sons, I finally understand it. You introduced me to books, poetry, and theater, and prodded me to explore my own feelings through words and imagery. You told me to listen to my own inner voice and feel experiences in my own way. "Honey, you have a gift, and one day you'll discover it," you said.

At the time, I had no idea what you meant.

When I turned thirteen, you bought me my first guitar, a nylon stringed Goya G-10 for less than a hundred dollars. It has aged as I have. The wood has dried out and there are subtle cracks in the fret board. This guitar, leaning against the worn couch in my living room, holds my memories and my past. It's a remnant of me that has traveled with me from my childhood home to college, to my first apartment, our starter home, and later to our larger home in the suburbs. It has never been far from my reach. It lifts me and consoles me. I'm connected to it season after season, as the pendulum of time swings over my shoulder. It'll always fit into my curves, and when I put my head against it, smelling its familiar smell, and strum it, it's like hearing your beating heart.

It took me thirty years and a glass of wine to finally grab my guitar and my sloppily handwritten songs and play before an audience. I felt like a snake shedding its skin. As I nervously walked to the front of that burnt red brick wall of a nearby coffee house, I had a flashback to the last time I performed. It was back in eighth grade girl's choir, when I had a mouthful of braces, hid behind long bangs, and held my arms tightly against my sides to hide the stains of perspiration. As I performed with the choir, you sat in the middle of the second row, beaming.

I've got to tell you, Mom, when I am on stage now, I am in a state of jubilant "guitar-ness." There's nothing like it. And nothing compares to having a fan approaching me afterwards and saying: "I haven't been moved like that by a song in a long time."

So, thank you Mom for all of your support, and for my perfect guitar. It was a perfect match for my dreams.

With all my love still,

Leslie
Hudson, Ohio

Leslie Wake is a freelance essayist and humor writer who is known as the "Guitar Lady" at the local children's hospital. She has three sons she is very proud of. In her spare time, she performs original songs at coffee houses.

Mom's Old-Fashioned Tomato Soup

BY ROBERT ROHLOFF

Dear Mom,

Coming from a family that did not hug and kiss much, I guess I turned out all right. Father was tough, but you were always gentle and understanding. I remember how you pampered me when I skinned my knee, and how you would wipe away my tears with your warm hand. Do you remember what you would say when performing those little acts of love? "Son, everything is going to be all right, because your mother loves you."

I still think of those words every time I think of you. Sure, we drifted apart when I hit those rebellious teenage years, but regardless, you accepted my long hair, my music, and my crazy clothes. You were always there to cheer for me at a baseball or basketball game, and even when I tried playing football. You were my number-one fan, Mom, and today I'm your number-one admirer.

Do you remember how we would laugh and laugh over those jigsaw puzzles we attempted? We would talk and laugh so hard that we would cry. Those silly puzzles with 5,000 pieces: I clearly remember the one with the clowns and balloons.

In the end, we discovered that the main clown was missing his big red nose! I know now why you had me do those puzzles. They taught me how to be patient, and it sure has come in handy during my career as a chef.

Yes, Mom, I became a chef thanks to you. It's because of you I learned how to crack an egg into a bowl without leaving any shell. My white sauce, tomato sauce, and hollandaise sauce are as good as yours were way back then. I wish you could taste my cream of tomato soup. It's just like yours. I use a bit of fresh dill in it just as you did. I even call it "Mom's Old-Fashioned Tomato Soup," and my customers all love it.

You gave me the opportunity to be all I could be. Thanks for taking the time to teach me the alphabet, how to write, and how to read. Today, I'm writing stories and sending them to publishers, and Mom, some of them are even being accepted, thanks to you. You gave me so many good experiences in my life to write about.

I cried when Father called to tell me you had departed this life. Father said it was from a hole in your heart—a hole in the biggest, warmest, loving heart that God had ever created.

Thank you for all the memories. For all the good times, all the skinned knees mended, tears dried, and most of all, thanks for simply being.

I don't know where to send this letter, Mom, so I just addressed it "heaven." I'm positive you will get it.

LOVE YOU, MOM,

Robert
Winnipeg, Manitoba, Canada

As a young man, Robert Rohloff hitchhiked across Canada and the United States, and credits that experience with his knowledge of human nature. He comes from Bohemian ancestry, which accounts for his Gypsy soul and his bohemian way of life.

In Your Eyes

BY DANA SMITH-MANSELL

Dear Mom,

I don't think I ever told you how much I admired your courage and strength. Time passes, and we involve ourselves with the business of days, often neglecting to acknowledge emotions of the heart. As you battled unknown illnesses for months prior to leaving this earth, you announced during one of our many conversations, "Some things just don't need to be said." At that precious moment I knew you didn't need to hear "I love you." You already knew.

While a letter cannot possibly address all you have done and given me, there were milestones that I reflect on fondly. You taught me how to tie my shoes. Hour after hour, day after day, you held me on the old oak rocker and patiently showed me: make one loop, wrap the other around, pull it through, and then tight. Your patience and pleasure in teaching me the little things in life were always apparent, as your smile and soft voice echo in my memory.

Your love of books helped me learn to read before I went to school. You would read story after story, and as you talked about characters your voice would fill with excitement and intrigue. You brought words and books to life, and created a love of words within me. We recited Robert Louis Stevenson's poems over and over again, and you showed pure delight when I was able to remember his works.

You also took great joy in watching me imitate others—even yourself! Your encouragement of my "performances" made me secure in attempting to make others laugh. You'd been an avid piano player since childhood, and you always encouraged me to explore music, dance, and art. You afforded me many opportunities to experience each discipline. No matter what I attempted, you always supported me, encouraged me, and made me feel that any dream was worthy. This love of art was one of your greatest gifts to me.

Mom, you never spoke a harsh word about anyone, even if it was warranted. I remember there were a few times when I thought a situation was inappropriate, and I wondered why you didn't say something. When I questioned you, you responded, "Rise above it." Even though that was difficult for your headstrong daughter to comprehend most times, with age I have come to develop a deeper understanding and appreciation of that phrase. You had a quote for everything, but the one that sticks with me most is "This too shall pass." This phrase saved me and saw me through more difficulties than I ever imagined. Thank you for giving me that understanding.

There were so many times during our excursions, conversations, and day-to-day living when I witnessed your courage. I admired it, and wanted to be *that* courageous. When Daddy passed, you were left with a teenager and an anxious preteen to raise alone. When serious illness struck, you battled for months and recovered. When others were rude and inconsiderate, you rose above it, and when I needed someone to talk to, you were always there to support, encourage, and guide me. That is what I miss the most.

You also developed my faith, encouraged my dreams, demonstrated determination in the face of adversity, and most of all, you nurtured compassion, honesty, courage, and hope. Thank you, Mom, for giving me the vision, the understanding, the courage, and the strength to dream. Because of you I became a special education professional, and was able to fulfill "our" dreams of being published. Your words and affection continue to give me the strength and courage to live each day to the fullest, and enjoy life and all its changes. I see the world because of you.

You were my advisor, my supporter, my friend, my rock, my sounding board, my example, and best of all, my mother. I'll always miss you.

Saying it now, Mom: "I love you."

ALL MY HEART,

Dana
Pottsville, Pennsylvania

Dana Smith-Mansell is a published author, poet, illustrator, and freelance writer. Her published works include Stop Bullying Bobby, Pink Jasper, Visions of Existence, *and* Sacred Intentions.

Love Letters

BY ANNE MAXWELL

Hi Mom,

I have wonderful news for you! Dad has finally moved from California to Oregon. I know, it's something the two of you had spoken about doing some ten years ago, and for one reason or another it just didn't happen then. But it has happened now, at least for Dad.

He arrived a few months ago with boxes upon boxes, filled with memories upon memories. It was an overwhelming endeavor for Dad to undertake, as I'm sure you know. The decision he made to finally move here had to be one of the most monumental and emotional decisions he has ever been presented with.

Before moving, he also faced opening long-ignored closets, kitchen cabinets, and drawers; going through old taped-up boxes; and then deciding what to sell, what to give away, and what to throw away. Opening memory upon memory, making decision after decision. I assure you, Mom, throughout the many long-distance telephone conversations I had with Dad during this time, I let him know which items I wouldn't want sold or tossed out, because they would find a new home with me. Dad was more than happy to comply with my sentimentality.

Dad arrived in Oregon a few days prior to the moving van, which was filled with furniture, artwork and collectibles, kitchenware, and memories. I can only imagine what Dad must've been thinking when the van pulled up, as he stood in the driveway of his new home awaiting the arrival of all his and your possessions.

Within minutes of the van arriving, I was there. Dad knew there wouldn't be a question of my helping him unpack. What I didn't know, Mom, is what I would find when I was helping him. Upon opening a certain box, I realized when I got to the bottom that it contained papers and photos. These items were things that Dad wouldn't want just anyone seeing. He had personally packed this box, not the moving company. I reached into the box, and there it was.

It was a plain piece of paper with typing on it. No date, no salutation, no signature. It caught my eye because it was typed, which was how you always wrote your letters. I still have every letter you sent to me after I moved away, every one of them typed and handsigned with "Much love, Mother." I couldn't help but start reading the letter.

Mom, it was the most beautiful letter I've ever read that you wrote. It was your love letter to Dad, the letter you intended him to find after you were gone. I was overwhelmed as I read your words, filled with sentiments of the love and life you had shared with Dad, how you knew you would once again be together, and your wishes for him to be happy and content with life after you were gone. Mom, you weren't sick. How did you know to write this love letter? I could only think while reading your extraordinary words that no matter what life would bring, you needed to once again tell Dad how much you loved him, loved your life together, how much you loved laughing together, and raising your children together.

I grew up in the home you and Dad made for us, knowing how much you two truly loved one another. My high school friends used to tell me how jealous they were of the relationship you had, because their parents never displayed such affection for one another. I grew up seeing you and Dad talk together every night, sharing the day's events, asking for and receiving advice on problems either of you may have had at work. You two shared a truly special and loving relationship, and I remember every day seeing you hug, kiss, and say "I love you." You held each other up high on well-deserved pedestals.

I don't know if I ever told you, but when I went for premarriage counseling with my fiancé Terry, the minister had us fill out questionnaires that were meant to give him insight on potential problem areas we could have in our marriage. After the minister had evaluated them, his only concern was the fact that both Terry and I held each other up too high on pedestals. What would happen if one of us slipped off that pedestal? My only response was we would help each other climb right back up on it.

You were the reason for my response, Mom. Because of you and your relationship with Dad, I was given one of the most beautiful gifts in my life. You taught me what it was to be in a loving, respectful, happy, secure relationship. It was what I wanted for myself, and I wouldn't settle for less.

The love letter you wrote to Dad, in those few paragraphs, summed up the loving lifetime you had together. When I read it, I was once again reminded of how much you taught me, and that I should still never settle for anything less.

MUCH LOVE,

Anne
Florence, Oregon

Anne Maxwell resides on the Oregon coast with her husband, where they ride Harleys with a vengeance. Her love of motorcycling is one of many passions she attributes to her parents.

Jewel in the Crown

By David R. Luhn

Dear Mother,

I know it's been a very long time since we've spoken. Time seems to have moved so quickly, and yet so silently, as if to purposely catch us unaware. I cannot believe it has been nearly eighteen years since we last saw each other, yet I can still see the radiance of your eyes and hear the softness of your words.

Though this world cares little of the separation thrust upon families and loved ones, it still provides simple pleasures of remembrance. Mother's Day quickly approaches and the new life that becomes apparent with spring reminds me of you. The beauty of its flowers is only surpassed by the beauty of your maternal love, and as I watch birds tirelessly provide nourishment for their young, I'm reminded of how unselfishly you provided for our family. It also brings to mind my shame in having not told you more often how I love you so very much and how I wish you could be here with me.

I often remember you hanging the wash in the dead of winter. When you came in from the cold, your hands were swollen and cracked. The preparation of daily meals also took its place in the line of ingratitude, as we children complained if we were asked to do the dishes. How little I had understood when you not only encouraged us, but insisted we finish our education and graduate. The sparkle in your eyes on graduation day made it all worthwhile.

It was also shamefully easy for me to take for granted your self-sacrifice. You had so many diverse roles of responsibility that you willingly took upon yourself. You were our mediator, accountant, decorator, holiday planner, and our source of joy and contentment. I count myself among the most fortunate of generations who had a stay-at-home Mom, but I wonder how many of your own dreams and aspirations were set aside? How often did I fail to remember the personal tragedies and burdens you had to bear? How many tears you must have silently cried. It is said that God counts the tears of women, and as such, he has surely provided an extra jewel in the crown of each Mother.

Mother, do not be surprised by these words, for mere words could never adequately reward the unconditional love you've shown me. It will always be my burden to bear knowing I failed to say "I love you" more often. And though I'm yet shackled in this world, in my soul I have no doubt that one day we shall see one another again, and I can once more say:

"MOTHER, I LOVE YOU."

David

Taneytown, Maryland

David R. Luhn has been a genealogist and historical researcher since 1984, and works as a freelance writer. His work entitled The Table appeared in the March/April 2006 issue of Everton's Genealogical Helper Magazine.

The Prodigal Granddaughter

By Sarah Wagner

Nan,

There are mothers by blood and mothers by deed, and you have been both in your time. Your daughter, my mother, was taken from us too soon, and you took up her burdens. You didn't have to take on an angry, bitter sixteen-year-old. You could have sent me to my father, but instead you chose to offer me stability.

I often felt that you were trying to replace my mom, and I rebelled as much against that as I did her death. I didn't want anyone else to be her, and I didn't want to be her daughter for anyone else. You moved into our house to care for me and my brother, and I was more concerned about preserving the sanctity of her domain than making you comfortable.

I knew everything and needed no one. I was angry and cruel, but you never once turned away from me. I pushed away from you and from everything I'd ever loved, but you wouldn't give up. You held fast even when my words had fangs. You allowed me to fall on my face and hit bottom, knowing it was the only way I would ever understand and ultimately grow up.

I would love to be able to say that I matured enough on my own to see my mistakes clearly, but I know it was the transition to motherhood that opened my eyes. When I held my son in my arms and looked into his face, I felt an overwhelming, all-consuming love for him. That's when I understood. My son opened the door for me to truly come home, and you opened your arms wide as I took the first tentative steps. I became the prodigal granddaughter.

At some point during my first year of motherhood, I realized everything you'd done after Mom died had been in my best interest. You did everything you could for me, and all you'd gotten was attitude. You moved out of your home and into my mother's so that my little brother and I could stay in the same school. You uprooted yourself from your friends and your husband—your entire support system—so that my brother and I wouldn't have to be uprooted. I can't imagine how hard it must have been for you to lose so much, only to deal with my misplaced rebellion.

Though I felt the weight of guilt and shame for all my many missteps, you never once threw it in my face. You could have, perhaps should have, and probably wanted to more than once. It wasn't as if I'd never left home, but it seemed to be water under the bridge.

You made me understand what unconditional love is. Forgiveness was never asked for but given wholly. Because of you, I have a definition of motherhood that I respect and hope to live up to. It would've been so easy for you to shut the door and lock me out. It wouldn't have been hard to ignore me, to forget me—but you didn't. I wish there were words enough for a mom like you, but I've discovered that there aren't. You might not be my mom, but you are my mom's mom, and I know she'd be proud of both of us—proud that you're her mom and that I'm her daughter, and proud that we never tried to replace her, but instead bonded because of her.

I don't tell you often enough that I love you. I flounder when it comes to buying you gifts because there's nothing that is worthy, that is enough to show my appreciation. Instead, I strive to achieve something great so that you'll be proud to know that I am yours.

I LOVE YOU,

Sarah

Weirton, West Virginia

Sarah Wagner lives in West Virginia with her family. When not writing, Sarah is assistant editor for Lily Literary Review *and runs a suggested reading list, The Imaginary Word. Her Web site is http://imaginaryword. betterfiction.com.*

HGACKTS

BY GLENDA STOVALL SCHOONMAKER

Dear Mom,

I can't wait to show you my new license plate because I know how much you like trying to decipher people's vanity plates. Mine is one of those puzzling words that compels other drivers to stay close enough to sniff the exhaust in an effort to figure it out. I was hoping that since my car has Arizona plates with cactus on it, it might make the meaning a little clearer, but ultimately that doesn't matter. What matters is that you will find it very humorous.

Remember how many times you've said I'm independent, stubborn, strong-willed, and hard-headed? Well, you know where I got that from, don't you? (And, we're not talking about Daddy!) It would amuse you to know that my husband very politely refers to me as a bulldog that sinks its teeth into something and never lets go. Canine though it may be, I find that to be a complimentary trait that I inherited from you.

When I was growing up, I wasn't very appreciative of your stronger personality traits. Even though you didn't start college until you were forty years old and I was in the sixth grade, you stubbornly strived for two bachelor's degrees. Buried in books at our metal kitchen table, you fervently studied your daily assignments. I wish I'd have understood then all that you were going through. I didn't realize that your gung-ho attitude about getting a college education was because you were afraid you might someday have to support my sister and me.

During those years you bought me nice clothes from the children's shop, but I can remember being ashamed that you seemed to wear ugly, unbecoming wraparound housedresses every day. I wish that children weren't so shallow. When I became a mom, I finally realized that you wanted the best for me and were willing to sacrifice your own clothing budget to make sure I had the best you could afford.

Recently, I was going through old family photographs and was shocked at how many pictures showed that throughout most of your life, you really did present a very fashionable appearance. There was even a picture of you, wearing a two-piece bathing suit, sitting next to Daddy on a beach in San Diego. It was taken when he was in the navy during World War II. I don't remember you ever allowing me to wear a two-piece bathing suit!

It has taken me years to be thankful that some of my traits are just like yours. Because of my inherited stubbornness, I was determined to have a good marriage and a loving relationship with my own kids. If you hadn't taught me to be so focused, I might never have had the marriage and relationship with my children that I now enjoy. Your tenacity was a gift.

So Dear Mom, in case you haven't figured it out, HGACKTS doesn't really have anything to do with Arizona. It's just my image of one cactus hugging another cactus without getting hurt. We've certainly had our moments, as two hard-headed women do, but through it all, you've taught me to never give up, to evaluate my words and actions, and above all to be more loving of others.

Giving you a hug from one cactus to another.

YOUR DAUGHTER,

Glenda
Lake Havasu City, Arizona

Glenda Stovall Schoonmaker is a motivational speaker, writer, and certified personality trainer. She lives in the desert southwest and has been married to her college sweetheart for thirty-six years. Her e-mail address is wordwardrobe@citlink.net.

Unconventional Wisdom

By Heather Skumatz

Dear Mom,

Did you know that when I was little, I sometimes worried that I was assigned the most unusual mom in the history of the world? What exactly was so unusual? Well for starters, you were older than my friends' parents, which was not exactly as fashionable then as it is now. If you had been famous, or been a lawyer or a doctor perhaps, the age difference between you and my peers' mothers would have been excusable. But you were no doctor—you were a farmer.

We also had a blended family. You were forty-something when my twin sister, Heidi, and I started kindergarten, and our stepdad was in his fifties. Our sister, Michelle, was a senior in high school. We also had two other sisters who were even older: one in college, and the other in the Peace Corps. These family quirks made us positively countercultural in the 1970s Midwest.

As such, I observed a few raised eyebrows, and I answered the nosy questions people asked as best I could, until I finally came to my own conclusions. My friends all had moms who looked the age of my sisters; therefore, my mom must be *old*. Good moms listened to the same songs their children did, they wore outfits that looked similar, and they always picked their children up from school.

You were a very different sort of mom. You told me—loudly and often—that it wasn't your job to be my friend. You listened to music that was already classified as "oldies," and you came to pick us up at school only if the bus driver died. When you did make a public appearance, you couldn't arrive inconspicuously, in the standard "mom uniform" consisting of a pressed blouse, jeans, and tasteful shoes. Instead, you wore flip-flops that showcased your grass-stained feet, and a western shirt tied at the waist over your bikini top. You also had varicose veins—but no one would have known had you not insisted on wearing your cutoff shorts!

At school, the teachers looked down the hall in surprise when they saw you drop your half-smoked cigarette back into the cellophane liner of your pack. You'd even greet the janitor, which was a big no-no for a parent of any student with dreams of being one of the cool kids.

Our classmates didn't come to play at our house because we were too far out in the country. My sister and I routinely told them it was too boring at our house, but if they insisted on coming, we'd spend as little time as possible, lest they realize we didn't actually have a shower in the bathroom. Instead, Heidi and I would beg you to take us to the beach, because we just didn't want to risk a deduction of coolness points by having little Buffy or Jessica step in one of the manure landmines in our yard.

So on those days, you'd rev up your 1967 Pontiac Catalina, drop us at the lake, and return at sundown. We might have a dollar each to last us all day, and if we forgot to pack our own lunch we were out of luck. We relied on the generosity of our friends or new acquaintances, or just went without, our stomachs rumbling underwater while our friends squealed. Unlike us, none of those girls had ever been swimming in a real lake, with real weeds and fish. They took their lifeguard-approved swimming lessons in the exceptionally sterile community pool.

You were the only mom I knew who could shoot a raccoon out of a tree, bury a cat killed on the road, and shift the H-pattern gearbox on a tractor. You were definitely the only mom I knew who "accidentally" let the air out of a trespassing fox hunter's tires. You told us later that you figured he couldn't have had more than one spare on that Jeep.

Mom, you taught me that following the major rules was good enough, and following them all was pathological. You taught me that kindness to all forms of life really does matter, and that it was okay to be the only girl playing football at recess as long as I was doing it because I loved to play, and not to impress the boys.

In short, you taught me that if one's motivations were sincere, the rest was just ornamental. I'm proud of my unconventional upbringing, Mom. Thanks for showing me, by example, what really matters in life.

LOVE,

Heather

Waupaca, Wisconsin

Heather Skumatz lives in central Wisconsin. She was educated at the University of Wisconsin-Stevens Point and works as a graphic designer.

When I Was in Sweden . . .

BY VICKI H. NELSON

Dear Mom,

It's been ten years since we last spoke, and as long as I can remember, we've had a bumpy relationship. There have been times when we haven't spoken for a year, but never has it been this long. Mom, I know you experienced a great deal of distress in your life, more than anyone should have had to endure. You had a traumatic childhood, full of heartache and sorrow, and carried many emotions from your painful memories into adulthood. And yet, while all that inner turmoil was going on inside of you, you remained strong.

You raised three children, cared for your handicapped mother who lived with us, and managed to keep a spotless home. We were always fed delicious homemade meals, like your vegetable soup, so creamy and flavorful. I can still taste your hot homemade biscuits, slathered and dripping with butter, their aroma carrying far into the alley behind our home. I've never been able to bake bread like you. You did a lot for your family, remaining solid the entire time.

From you, I learned strength.

As a child, you received little compassion from your parents, though they knew your brothers were abusing you. And yet, Mom, you were so compassionate to me when I was ill or injured. As I'm sure you know, I faked being sick many times just so I could stay home and be pampered by you. I remember one time when I fell on the ice, landing square on my elbow, which resulted in my arm being placed in a sling. Since I was a self-conscious teenager, you took the time to comb my hair in place, making sure I looked good for school.

And remember what an ordeal it was when I had my wisdom teeth removed? I was so terrified that I passed out in the doctor's chair before they even had a chance to give me anesthesia. You stayed with me through it all, and afterward, when I was sick to my stomach, you brought me all the ice cream, pudding, and soup I could eat. I still remember that worried look on your face, and when my own sons were sick, I loved caring for them the way you cared for me.

From you, I learned compassion.

My friends adored you. They called you "Mom." You were kind to them, fed them, and treated them as your own, but most of all, they loved your funny stories. Remember your Sweden stories? They always started out with "When I was in Sweden . . . " and would continue on to relate some grand adventure you experienced while you were there. They cracked us up. The best part was, you were never in Sweden, though from your stories, even I wondered if you hadn't been there!

From you, I learned to be a storyteller.

Do you remember our Christmas bake-offs? We would spend the entire day baking cookies. One year we attempted meringue doves, but they ended up looking like funky UFOs. We laughed till we cried and fell to the floor. I still have the picture my husband took of us. One year my kids helped us. I don't remember getting much baking done, but I do remember the flour that coated our hands, the floor, and the countertops. That was the best flour fight!

From you, I learned to have fun.

Mom, we may not always think the same; in fact, it seems that you and I tend to disagree more than we agree. But one thing I think we can agree on is that you taught me a lot, and for that I will always be thankful. No matter where you are at this point in your life, you will always be a part of me.

LOVE,
YOUR DAUGHTER,

Vicki

Beaverton, Oregon

Vicki Nelson was raised in Minnesota. A writer, she now resides in Oregon with her husband and two sons.

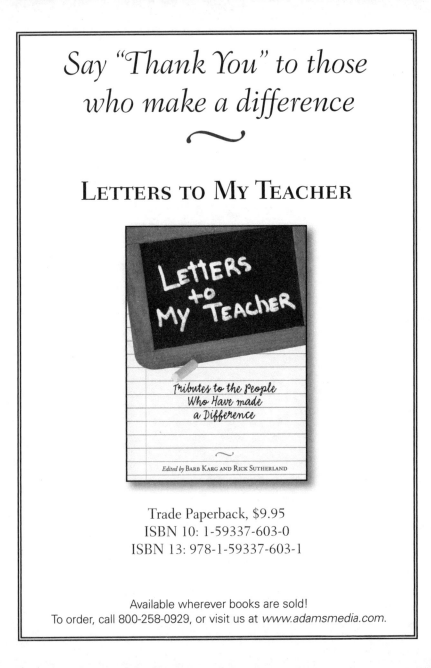